The Real Employee Handbook

A Top Lawyer Reveals What You Need To Know - And What Your Boss Won't Tell You

Randy Freking

The Real Employee Handbook

A Top Lawyer Reveals What You Need To
Know - And What Your Boss Won't Tell You

Randy Freking

The Real Employee Handbook

A Top Lawyer Reveals What You Need To Know - And What Your Boss Won't Tell You

Copyright © 2012 by Randolph H. Freking

Printed in the United States of America.

For information: Randolph H. Freking, Esq., Freking and Betz, LLC, 525 Vine Street, Cincinnati, Ohio 45202; randy@frekingandbetz.com

Library of Congress Cataloging-In-Publication Data

ISBN: 147745134X

ISBN 13: 9781477451342

Dedication

I dedicate this book to every employee in the United States who tries to balance the all-encompassing demands of his or her family, his or her employer, and his or her job.

Acknowledgments

I would like to acknowledge the individuals who assisted me in the creation of this book. Most importantly, Susan Bradley of Eagan, Minnesota, spent countless hours editing my book and asking substantive questions that improved the quality of the information presented. In addition, Bill Thompson of Cincinnati provided valuable editing assistance from his many years as a copy editor for the *Cincinnati Enquirer.* Paul H. Tobias, the founder of the National Employment Lawyers Association and co-founder of the National Employee Rights Institute (now called Workplace Fairness), has been my mentor since 1990, when I began my private practice representing employees. Paul graciously reviewed the text and provided valuable insight to me as he has done the last 22 years.

Kelly Mulloy Myers, one of my six law partners, devoted her attention to the substance of the information contained in this book and provided valuable assistance.

Karen Pavy, my administrative assistant, patiently assisted with the seemingly never-ending modifications to the text and formatting of the book.

Stuart Kunkler of Cincinnati, Ohio, designed the cover.

Last but not least, all of my partners, colleagues, members of the National Employment Lawyers Association and Workplace Fairness, and our clients who have provided much of the practical, day-to-day advice that is important whenever considering various workplace issues.

Contents

Part 5 Understanding Your Rights as an Employee 51

Introduction

If you work for a living, regardless of whether you are a "blue collar" hourly employee or a "white collar" salaried worker, this book is for you. It contains important information that your prospective, current, or former employer does not want you to know, including the basics of your rights and obligations in the workplace, as well as practical tips on how to level the playing field regarding issues that arise every day on the job.

Your job is likely one of the three most important aspects of your life, along with your family and your religion, in whatever order of priority you choose. Despite the central importance of one's job, most people don't fully understand the rules that define their employment, or know what to do when the relationship with their employer sours.

All too often, employees who have questions about their rights at work rely on their not-so-well-intentioned bosses, or on well-meaning but misinformed co-workers, friends, and family members. For a variety of reasons, not the least of which is the complexity of employment law, the information provided by these people cannot often be trusted. In addition, when employees search various HR websites for answers to their employment questions, they usually become more confused than they were to begin with. The difficulty in obtaining clear, reliable information leaves employees with many questions, such as the following:

- Do I have any rights in the workplace even if I am told I am "employed at will"?
- What should I do when I receive a warning or a poor performance evaluation that I believe to be unfair?
- Can my boss fire me without any warning?
- Can an employer require me to disclose my social media passwords?
- Am I entitled to overtime pay even if I am paid a salary?

- If I quit or am fired due to no fault of my own, can my current employer enforce the non-competition agreement I signed when I was hired?
- What forms of discrimination are unlawful?
- What are my rights if I think I am the victim of discrimination?
- What are my rights if I am working in a hostile work environment?
- Am I protected if I complain about unfair treatment?
- When should I seek legal help for problems on the job?

You will find answers to these and many other common questions in this easy-to-read book, along with practical tips to help you protect your job and enforce your rights.

It bears mentioning at the outset that your chances of continuing to draw a paycheck are much higher if you know your rights and employ successful strategies to keep your job, since the odds for a favorable outcome are not in your favor if you entrust your case to the justice system. Seeking legal remedy after a job loss is less than ideal because of the many twists and turns that can ensue, as well as the very real possibility that a decision will not go in your favor. Even if you have been undeniably wronged in your employment, your outcome will be significantly impacted by factors such as whom you or the company retains as counsel, your ability to afford a legal battle, the attitude of the company toward a peaceful settlement, characteristics of the court system and judges in your jurisdiction, and ultimately your luck of the draw with potential jurors. Given these many variables, it is wiser for you to know your rights now rather than plan on winning a legal challenge down the long road of litigation.

We recommend that you read each of the short explanations in this book to fully understand the employment relationship, but if you seek information on a specific issue, the topics are organized so you can find what you need in a matter of minutes.

Please note that this book is intended to provide information about the rights and responsibilities of employees in the private, non-union workforce. Occasional references are made to unionized employees and to non-private, or public, employment situations, but considerations for employees in those settings often differ from those affecting the private workforce.

Since every employment situation is unique, many facts must be considered before you can determine if your company has violated the law. This book is designed to provide basic and useful information about your rights as an employee. It will help you determine whether to seek the advice of an employment attorney about your particular situation. It is not intended as legal advice and should not be construed as such.

Part 1 Job Security

Why You Can't Be Disciplined or Fired "For Any Reason"

The Employment-at-Will Myth

"Employment at will" is an often repeated phrase that is, in many ways, as outdated as the factories of the late 1800s that spawned this legal doctrine.

The employment-at-will doctrine literally means that, unless you have a contract of employment providing job security rights, an employer may discipline or fire you for a good reason, a bad reason—even an immoral or unethical reason—or no reason at all. Thus, under this doctrine, an employer can lawfully fire an employee because of his race, his age, or any of the other exceptions discussed in this book.

First, it is beneficial to discuss what employment at will is *not*. The employment-at-will doctrine has nothing to do with unionized employees who have bargained for "just cause" protection against unfair employment decisions. Similarly, the term is often used erroneously to imply that non-union employees have no rights against wrongful discharges. In addition, some people confuse the phrase "right-to-work state" with employment at will, and incorrectly use the terms interchangeably. We will address "right to work" considerations later in Part 1.

According to legal scholars, the policy of employment at will began to appear in the 1880s as part and parcel of the *laissez faire* philosophy of the times. Under the *laissez faire* approach, the federal, state, and local governments intervened very little in issues relating to business and commerce, and instead allowed the free market to dictate employment policies. Adoption of the employment-at-will doctrine occurred during the second phase (the so-called Technological Revolution) of the Industrial Revolution, which ran from the late 1800s to World War I. This doctrine afforded mutual rights to employers and employees, in that employers could terminate employees at any time, and employees could quit whenever they saw fit to do so. Although employment at will afforded employers considerable power over the fate of their employees, it also enabled employees to demand better treatment at times when laborers were scarce and employers couldn't afford to lose them. The policy has since fallen out of favor with modern legal scholars, many of whom question the authenticity of the purported origins of the rule.

The employment-at-will policy was tolerable in the late 19th century because jobs in that era were less technical and required less education, meaning that employees could move easily from one job to another.

Nonetheless, the doctrine implicitly encourages employers not to care or worry about the fairness of employment decisions.

The Historical Decline of Employment at Will

Not surprisingly, the adoption and expansion of employment at will coincided with the birth of the labor movement in the United States. Workers in various industries sought ways to band together to protect themselves from unfavorable treatment and arbitrary termination by employers. Unionization allowed individuals to unite in order to bargain for better working conditions and job protection, with the collective threat of a strike if fair terms could not be negotiated. The primary benefit of organizing employees was the effective abolishment of the employment-at-will policy in unionized workplaces. In contrast to the *laissez faire* right of a company to unilaterally terminate an employment relationship for any or no reason, unions won the right of job security for their members by requiring employers to show "just cause" before disciplining or firing any employee of the organized company.

Participation in unions has waxed and waned in the U.S. during the past century. According to U.S. Census figures, 4.2% of nonagricultural workers were union members in 1900, with membership peaking at nearly 35% of the labor force by the mid-1950s. Union participation has declined steadily since that time, such that by 2010, only 11.9% of American workers belonged to unions.

The decline in union membership has been most visible in private sector unions. According to a January 27, 2012, release by the United States Bureau of Labor Statistics, only 6.9% percent of private sector wage and salary workers were members of a union in 2011. Participation in public sector unions has remained stronger, as 37% of government employees were union members in 2011.

If you are employed in a unionized workplace, you likely have a grievance and arbitration process to challenge unfair discipline or discharge. This right is independent of most of the "rights" described in this book, so the union representing employees may choose to challenge discipline through the grievance and arbitration process or, if unionized employees believe some unlawful motive exists for the company's actions, they may also proceed through the judicial system to enforce their rights. Many employees can pursue both routes.

Legislative Exceptions to Employment at Will

Not coincidentally, as the doctrine of employment at will has diminished in recent years, legislation to protect employees' rights has expanded. A host of laws has been developed to increase job security by prohibiting employer conduct that previously would have been perfectly acceptable under the employment-at-will doctrine.

Consider the following federal law exceptions to the employment-at-will doctrine:

- Title VII of the Civil Rights Act (1964)
- The Pregnancy Discrimination Act (1978)
- The Equal Pay Act (1963) and the Lilly Ledbetter Act (2009)
- Section 1981 of the Civil Rights Act (1866)
- The Age Discrimination in Employment Act (1967)
- The Older Workers Benefit Protection Act (1986)
- The Uniformed Services Employment and Reemployment Rights Act (1994)
- The Occupational Safety and Health Act (1970)
- The Americans with Disabilities Act (1990)
- The Rehabilitation Act (1973)
- The Family and Medical Leave Act (1993)
- The Fair Labor Standards Act (1938)
- The Employee Retirement Income Security Act (1974)
- The Worker Adjustment and Retraining Notification Act (1988)
- The National Labor Relations Act (1935)
- The Consumer Credit Protection Act (1968)
- The Juror Protection Act (1978)
- Genetic Information Non-Discrimination Act (2008)
- Section 1983 of the Civil Rights Act (1870)
- The Whistleblower Protection Act (1989)
- The False Claims Act (1863)
- The Sarbanes-Oxley Act (2002)
- The Dodd-Frank Act (2010)
- Environmental whistleblower laws (7 acts in various years)
- Food Safety Modernization Act (2010)

Consider, also, that many states, either legislatively or judicially, have created exceptions to employment at will in the following areas:

- Sexual orientation and preference
- Transgender discrimination
- Breach of contract
- Promissory estoppel
- Breach of public policy
- Negligent or intentional interference with the employment relationship
- Defamation
- Intentional infliction of emotional distress
- False imprisonment
- Invasion of privacy
- Fraud
- Assault
- Negligence

As this list indicates, myriad laws address employment issues. Although the vast majority of these laws do not apply to every particular situation, evaluation of challenged employment decisions should include the possibility that one or more of the exceptions above, as well as others that are developing at the federal and state level, might be applicable.

Why Some Lawyers Still Invoke Employment at Will

Unfortunately, even well-intentioned lawyers remember the employment-at-will doctrine from law school and still invoke it today without explaining the various exceptions:

- "You probably have no basis to challenge your termination because [insert state] is an employment-at-will state."
- "It's likely you cannot do anything about your hostile work environment because you are employed at will."

This kind of advice from lawyers borders on malpractice, given the implication that somehow the employment-at-will doctrine is as alive and well today as it was during the Industrial Revolution of the nineteenth century. These lawyers—hopefully not employment lawyers—seemingly forget that Congress and the various states have enacted a plethora of exceptions to the doctrine.

Yes, it was legal during the early twentieth century to fire someone for trying to form a union, for being African American, for being "too old," and so on. It was legal because "employment at will" meant you could be fired for a good reason, a bad reason, or no reason at all. This is hardly the case anymore and you should consult an employment lawyer—not a tax lawyer or an estate lawyer—if you have one or more questions about your rights.

Non–employment lawyers often fail to ask the right questions. They tend to ask about the stated reason for the company's action and, perhaps, whether the client thinks he or she was treated in a discriminatory manner.

- "Did you do what they said you did?"
- "Do you think they committed {age, race, sex] discrimination?

Although these are important questions, they only touch the surface.

More inquiry is necessary for two reasons. First, while the company's articulated explanation is important when considered in a vacuum, even a good reason can be discriminatory or lead to some other exception to employment at will. If you are fired because you missed work without calling in to report your absence, this might sound like a good reason to justify the company's actions. However, what if other employees were not fired for similar infractions? What if you had reported an OSHA violation recently?

The second reason is that you, like most people who believe they were treated unfairly, do not want to scream "discrimination," but you believe that there are laws requiring just cause even in a non-union context. Moreover, you likely do not know enough about possible legal theories to form a valid opinion as to whether some exception to the employment-at-will policy provides you with rights. Thus, simply asking, "Do you think you were fired because you are a woman?" will likely result in the answer "No."

Instead, what you should examine is whether you were treated differently than others, or differently than company policy provides, or whether you were disciplined or fired after engaging in some type of "protected" activity that shields you from unlawful retaliation.

Everyone Is Protected by One or More Laws

The many exceptions to employment at will have effectively disabled and devoured the rule. You may believe you are employed at will if you aren't protected by an individual employment contract or a union's collective bargaining agreement, but everyone is protected to some degree against unfair, arbitrary, or capricious termination. It's just that some people can utilize more of the exceptions to employment at will than can others.

The Limited Meaning of "Right-to-Work" Laws

"Right-to-work state" is a phrase that lawyers hear from non-union employees, either as some sort of misquote of employment at will, or in the context of non-compete agreements the employee wants to negate.

- "I heard this is a right-to-work state and that I have no rights. Is that true?"
- "I signed a non-compete agreement when I was hired, but this is a 'right-to-work' state. So I can go work for a competitor, right?"

Both are used in the wrong context and both assume the wrong answer.

"Right-to-work" laws are in place in 23 states, with Indiana in 2012 becoming the most recent state to enact such a law, and the first state to do so in more than a decade. Indiana is the only state in the Midwestern manufacturing belt to have passed such a law.

As a practical matter, right-to-work laws are only important to unionized workers, as they bar unions—in collective bargaining agreements negotiated with companies—from requiring non-union members to pay fees for representation, even though the non-union members are entitled to the benefits of the agreements. Right-to-work laws mean nothing beyond the issue of whether all unionized employees must pay union dues.

The phrase is also used erroneously by people who say, "I have a right to work and my former employer cannot deny me that right even though I signed a non-competition agreement." Although it is true that non-competition agreements are often overly broad and may be subject to judicial modifications, they are almost always enforceable to some degree. They never totally deny you a right to find a job; they just limit the range of options in your job search. A right-to-work law has no relevance in the interpretation of a non-competition agreement.

Simply put, right-to-work laws have nothing to do with job security or the enforceability of non-compete agreements. For unionized employees, they affect nothing other than the issue of whether you can be compelled to pay union dues.

Part 2

Why It Matters How Many Employees Work
for Your Company and the State
in Which You Are Employed

The Size of Your Employer Matters

In employment rights, size matters because many smaller employers are not subject to all of the federal or state laws granting employees certain rights. Later in this book, you will learn the minimum number of employees required before an employer is covered by certain laws.

For example, only employers with at least 20 employees must adhere to the federal Age Discrimination in Employment Act. Other laws, such as the Employee Polygraph Protection Act, apply to virtually all employers.

Tip: It would be wrong to assume that no law applies to you if you work for a small employer not subject to federal employment laws. Allow an employment lawyer an opportunity to evaluate all of the available exceptions to employment at will if you believe you are being treated unfairly or have been in the past.

Your State Matters

The state in which you work is important in determining the scope of rights and remedies available to you. In some states, your rights and remedies may exceed those set as a minimum by Congress. Many state legislatures have passed employment laws modeled after federal law, but with broader coverage in some instances and greater potential liability for an employer.

As an example, Ohio age discrimination laws cover employers with only four or more employees, thus greatly increasing the number of small businesses that cannot lawfully treat older employees differently than younger employees. Federal age discrimination law applies only if an employer has at least 20 employees.

Thus, if an older worker is fired in Ohio while working for a company with 10 employees (10 fewer than the federal threshold), the worker can only assert rights protecting her from age discrimination under Ohio law. If this is the only legal claim, she can most likely pursue the matter only in an Ohio court. It should be noted that Ohio law does not usually allow a successful employee to recover attorneys' fees and costs as part of her remedy, unlike federal age discrimination law; however, Ohio grants some greater remedies than are available under the federal age discrimination law, such as emotional distress damages.

North Carolina, on the other hand, has not passed an anti-discrimination law. So, if an older worker there is fired on the basis of age while working for a company with fewer than 20 employees, the employee has no legal recourse. In effect, employers with fewer than 20 employees can lawfully treat older and younger workers differently.

Tip: Since your state may afford you greater rights than have been granted by Congress, it is wise to contact an employment attorney in your state when questions arise. Even if you have a friend or relative who is a lawyer, consulting with a lawyer you know only makes sense if she is licensed to practice law in your state and is knowledgeable about your state's employment laws.

The Forum of the Court Matters

The laws of your state are also important in determining your choice of the forum in which to bring your claim. For example, if you have a right to be free from sex discrimination under both federal law and state law, you might have the option of choosing to enforce that right in either a state court (forgoing the federal claim for strategic purposes) or simply proceeding in federal court under both federal and state law.

Choice of forum might have a dramatic impact on one's likelihood of success. A major reason relates to the potential judges who might oversee the case. Although most cases are assigned randomly within a particular court system (state or federal), attorneys may feel more comfortable—and be more likely to succeed—with the judges from one pool or the other.

Suffice it to say, the judge—whether a state or federal judge— who oversees a case is a critical participant in the proceeding even if a jury ultimately renders the verdict. Although you might think that all judges apply and interpret the law in a similar manner, the gray areas of most employment laws and various evidentiary rules are open to vastly different interpretations.

Likewise, your choice of forum will have an impact on the set of jurors to decide your claims. If you work in Colorado, for example, the potential jurors come from the entire state if you file a lawsuit in federal court because Colorado has a single federal district court based in Denver. If you live in Boulder County and choose to proceed under state law in a state court based in Boulder County, however, prospective jurors will be limited to residents of Boulder County. Depending on the nature of your case, the composition of the jury can greatly influence your outcome.

Tip: If you are considering retaining an employment lawyer, ask if she practices in both state and federal court and is familiar with strategic considerations in deciding where to file your case.

Part 3

The Basics of Lawful and Unlawful Discrimination

What Is Discrimination?

First, let's look at what it means to discriminate. The Merriam Webster Dictionary defines "discriminate" as "to make a difference in treatment or favor on a basis other than individual merit." It provides as an example, "to discriminate in favor of your friends."

People discriminate all the time. We choose something or someone over another based on factors other than merit. We might say, "I think I'll patronize that restaurant even though the service is not good, since the owner seems to be struggling." This might be unfair to the better restaurant next door, but it is certainly legal.

In the workplace, some confusion has been created by references in the media and popular culture to "wrongful discharge" cases. A headline pronounces, "60-year-old ex-IBM worker wins wrongful discharge suit," implying that the employee won because he was wrongfully dismissed. A more accurate headline would say, "Former IBM worker wins age discrimination suit." If the ex-employee only proved that he was wrongfully dismissed, he likely would have lost his case because he must also prove that the company considered his age when making the decision or treated him differently than younger co-workers.

Tip: Always remember the issue in legal cases challenging a job termination is not whether the decision was wrong or unfair. The issue usually focuses on the employer's motive in making the decision. Many unfair dismissals are legal.

Not All Discrimination on the Job Is Illegal

The word "discrimination" is commonly, but sometimes improperly, used in the employment context regarding what conduct constitutes unlawful discrimination. Employees often complain that someone or some group of people is being favored in the workplace, resulting in differences in treatment. Not all discrimination in the workplace is unlawful, however. For example, when one company acquires another, there is often a perception that the managers of the acquiring company favor the managers and employees in their organization over the supervisors and workers of the acquired company:

- "I was better qualified than Ahern to run the IT department of the merged company, but the operations VP chose Ahern because they had worked together before."
- "They are giving preference to employees who worked for their company before the merger."

Another common perception is that friends of a decision maker receive preferential treatment:

- "I was chosen for the layoff because I didn't socialize with my boss as much as Laura did, and my boss kept her even though I had better performance reviews."
- "I didn't get a performance bonus as high as Bob because Bob is buddies with the manager who is deciding how to distribute the bonuses."

A third set of examples involves employees being preferred because they are "brown-nosers."

- "Jen got the job because she always agrees with the boss, Sue, even when it's obvious Sue is wrong."
- "Becky was promoted because she always took on the boss's pet projects and bragged about her accomplishments."

Are the above examples unfair? Perhaps, since at least some employment decisions are being made on factors other than merit. But are they illegal? Read on.

Tip: *Most employment cases are heavily dependent on an analysis of many facts about how your workplace has handled similar cases. Maintaining a diary is a good idea and should include as much information about your co-workers as you know. For example, most employment lawyers will want demographic information about the workforce—the age, race, gender, and other protected characteristics of each of your co-workers.*

What Is Wrongful Discharge?

"Wrongful discharge" is an umbrella term commonly used to refer to *unlawful* discharge. The two phrases are not synonymous with each other, however. When evaluating your situation, it is important to focus on factors that are unlawful as opposed to factors that might be unfair or wrong (although most successful unlawful discharge cases have a good dose of unfairness mixed in with the unlawful consideration). By definition, unlawful treatment is "wrongful," but not all wrongful treatment is unlawful.

Unlawful Employment Discrimination Basics

Most unlawful employment actions are born out of decisions or policies that are, at least in part, based upon protected characteristics identified in laws or statutes passed by state legislatures or Congress. These laws generally prohibit an employer from considering "protected characteristics" such as race, gender, age, or disability in employment decisions that are "adverse" to an applicant or employee.

Other unlawful employment actions arise out of violations or disrespect of various rights created for certain other persons, including veterans, people who need to care for their own or others' serious medical conditions, and people who oppose unlawful conduct or support others' opposition to unlawful conduct. These laws are described in Parts 7 and 8 of this book.

Since the 1960s, federal courts have grappled with the issue of proof in discrimination cases, since discrimination is rarely admitted, and most situations need to be evaluated based on conflicting circumstantial evidence favoring either the employee or the employer.

In the next six topical sections, we will review the most common legal theories underlying claims of unlawful employment discrimination and the applicable manner of analysis:

- Unlawful disparate treatment
- Unlawful retaliation based on protected speech
- Unlawful retaliation based on conduct
- Unlawful failure to accommodate a disability or religious belief
- Unlawful interference
- Unlawful disparate impact

Unlawful Disparate Treatment

Unlawful disparate treatment is the most commonly litigated form of employment discrimination. It is sometimes misunderstood because of its shorthand description as simply "disparate treatment," which only tells you that there was a difference in treatment. *Unlawful* disparate treatment looks to the <u>motive</u> for the difference in treatment and whether the <u>motive</u> is based on a protected characteristic.

- "I'm the best female accountant the company ever had and they replaced me with some woman they just hired."
- "Can you believe they laid me off at age 50 after I've worked 15 years for the company, but they kept that guy they just hired and he's 10 years older than I am?"
- "I was denied a promotion and they gave it to another African American who isn't nearly as qualified as I am."

If these explanations are all we know, the person certainly might be able to show disparate treatment, but will lack proof of *unlawful* disparate treatment. The female accountant will have trouble proving she was fired because of her gender if she was replaced by a woman. In the second example, the older employee will not prove unlawful discrimination based on age if he's treated differently than a worker who is older than he is. Likewise, while the African American may have been treated unfairly in the promotion decision, it's hard to claim race discrimination if the preferred candidate is also African American.

On the other hand, workplace situations are rarely as simple as conveyed in the quotes above. An attorney might learn that the fired female accountant was substantially older than the newly hired woman, indicating there might be proof of age discrimination. If the 50-year-old who was replaced by someone older is a minority, there might be evidence of race discrimination. In the event that the fired African American had a serious disability, a disability discrimination claim might be warranted.

Alleged unlawful disparate treatment claims use an analytical framework recognized by the United States Supreme Court in its landmark decision, *McDonnell Douglas vs. Green*. From an employee's standpoint, you must first be able to prove four elements of such a claim, the first three of which are the least complicated.

First, you must be in one or more "protected classes" identified by Congress. These protected classes are described in Part 7. It should be noted that disgruntled employees often fall into a number of protected classes. For example:

- Are you over 40 years of age (the age-protected class)?
- Are you female or male? (Yes, men are also protected against sex discrimination!)
- Are you a member of a particular religion?
- Were you pregnant or returning from a maternity leave?
- Do you suffer from a disability?

Second, you must be able to establish that you were qualified for your job. Most employees with any significant length of service can establish this element, and the courts have applied a low threshold of proof on this requirement.

Third, you must prove you are the victim of some type of "adverse action." An employment termination is obviously an adverse action, as is the denial of a promotion. However, other actions are trickier to ascertain and need to be carefully analyzed, such as an undesirable transfer, an undesirable working shift change, or a disadvantageous revision of duties.

The fourth element of the *McDonnell Douglas* framework is a frequent focus of employment litigation. In the termination context, you can satisfy the fourth element by proving that you were replaced by someone outside your particular protected class or, in the age discrimination context, someone substantially younger. So, for example, if you are female and claim sex discrimination, one way to satisfy the fourth element is simply by showing that, after you were fired, a male replaced you. In the age discrimination context, a worker over age 40 shows this by proving she was replaced by someone significantly younger (defined in most jurisdictions as 7–8 years), not necessarily someone outside the "class," because such an interpretation would be disadvantageous to the oldest employees.

If you don't have proof of a replacement to establish the fourth element, the analysis does not end, but simply becomes more subtle or complex. The fourth element can also be proved by other circumstantial evidence, such as proof that others not in your protected class were not discharged for a similar offense, or statistical proof of some unlawful pattern of conduct (for example, in a diverse workforce, the last 10 employees fired were in the same protected class). There are other types of proof that depend on the particular circumstances.

Establishing these four elements of disparate treatment claims means that the employee can satisfy the *prima facie,* or "at first glance," case of illegal discrimination. Under federal employment laws, this means that you have enough evidence to require the company to explain its conduct. So, if you are in a protected class (as everyone is), are or were qualified for your job, are subject to an adverse action, and have evidence that you were treated differently than, or replaced by, one or more persons outside your class, you have enough evidence to require the company to explain its decision. If you cannot establish a *prima facie* case, the company is not legally required to explain its action.

Assuming a *prima facie* showing can be made, the analytical process then looks to the explanation provided by the company to defend its decision. Technically, the employer must articulate a legitimate, non-discriminatory reason or reasons for whatever adverse action it took in the particular case. This is a low threshold and every company can meet this burden because an employer always believes that it has some good reason for its decision.

The question then becomes, essentially, whether the reason stated by the company is true or is a pretext, or cover-up, for unlawful conduct.

A successful disparate treatment claim requires proof of both the *prima facie* case and whether the company is trying to hide an unlawful discriminatory motive. Sometimes, a jury concludes that an employee met the *prima facie* requirements and proved the employer was lying about its motive, and yet finds that some other lawful motive was the <u>real</u> motive, such as the favored employee being a friend of the decision maker.

Most disparate treatment cases that proceed to trial, however, will ultimately be decided on the question of whether the employer's stated reasons can be believed or whether they mask the company's true intent, i.e., to treat a protected employee differently on the basis of that protected characteristic.

Tip 1: *It is not necessary to prove that an employer treats all members in a protected group unfairly. Employment lawyers may hear from the company or potential client that the company "has a lot of {insert protected class} and they are still employed, so how can the company be guilty of discrimination?" This is not a defense. The question is whether the employer treated you differently because of your protected characteristic.*

***Tip** 2: The protected status of the decision maker is not determinative. For example, just because a female decided to fire a woman does not mean there was not a sex discrimination bias. Members of a protected class are perfectly capable of treating others in the same protected class differently.*

Unlawful Retaliation Based on Speech

Unlawful retaliation claims are the most straightforward, and easiest to understand, of all employment cases. These claims tend to scare employers, because it is difficult for a company to have them dismissed before trial. In addition, they are viewed as more problematic than most other types of cases once they go to trial.

In essence, retaliation cases involve the simple question of whether the employer reacted negatively to an employee's exercise of a protected right. Proving "retaliation" by your employer is not enough; you must first have engaged in some protected speech (or conduct, described next), and there must be a link between your protected speech or conduct and the retaliatory act.

Consider the following:

- "My boss canned me because I complained when he gave me an unfavorable appraisal. The evaluation ignored half of my achievements."
- "I was disciplined after I went above my supervisor and complained to her boss. The boss agreed with me, but my supervisor thought I should have followed the chain of command."
- "The company fired me because I questioned the way the marketing department made its budget forecast. It was all wrong."

If these statements are true, it seems like the employee was the victim of retaliation. However, if this is the entire story, the retaliation is not illegal because each employee's speech was not "protected" by a specific law.

In order to be protected from retaliation for speech, the employee must oppose some unlawful action or practice by the employer. Several federal laws provide such protection, and the most common complaints pertain to discriminatory conduct protected by Title VII or conduct protected by various whistleblower laws under state and federal law. An example of the first type of complaint might be, "You are discriminating against me because of my age [or another protected classification]." An example of the second type might be, "You are violating federal safety laws."

This type of protected speech can be oral, such as remarks made to a supervisor, or written, such as a formal rebuttal to a performance review.

Assuming you have engaged in protected speech and have then suffered some adverse action, the question becomes whether you have evidence of some "causal connection" between your speech and the adverse action. A causal connection is sometimes shown by timing, e.g., how soon discipline occurs after a complaint, or by showing that the employer's stated reason is pretextual and designed to mask the retaliatory motive.

Tip: *Employees who complain are often viewed as problem employees. Before you complain about an employer's conduct, consider whether you have protection against retaliation. If you do not, be aware that retaliation for speaking up may be lawful.*

Sometimes it is better to stay silent if you do not trust your boss to receive the complaint as it is intended. A job buys groceries; simply standing on principle does not.

Unlawful Retaliation Based on Conduct

Federal laws also protect employees who engage in certain conduct that is protected. These cases usually involve either making a formal claim of discrimination, exercising a protected right, or participating in another employee's case as a witness.

The first type usually involves a person who has made a formal complaint to a federal agency charged with enforcing various employment laws. For example, if you file a charge with the U.S. Equal Employment Opportunity Commission alleging that your company has discriminated against you, you have engaged in protected conduct. An employer is prohibited from taking adverse action against you because of that conduct.

The second type of conduct that garners protection against retaliation is the exercise of a protected right. Perhaps the most common example involves a person who decides to take a leave from work under the Family and Medical Leave Act, described in Part 7. Under that law, an employer is prohibited from taking any action against an employee for exercising that right.

The least common type of protected conduct involves participating in another employee's claim. Such participation could come in the form of serving as a witness in support of a claim, or providing some other assistance to a person making a claim.

Tip 1: It is critical that you document activities in the workplace that provide you with job protection. For example, if a co-worker claims discrimination and you support that co-worker, obtain and keep a copy of any statement you provide or maintain a record of any oral statement. Keep any such paper trail at home, away from the employer's property.

Tip 2: You do not need to be correct about the content of either your speech or your conduct. What is required is that you have a good faith belief that the action you are protesting (either on your own or by supporting another) is unlawful. Thus, if you make a good faith claim that you are the victim of discrimination, you are protected from retaliation even if you do not ultimately establish that you were correct. These laws allow you to raise issues of concern in good faith and recognize that you may not have complete or accurate information.

Unlawful Failure to Accommodate

In addition to a right to be free from discrimination, persons with disabilities and persons with sincere religious beliefs are entitled to "reasonable accommodation." If you are in one of these classes and need some type of relief in order to perform your job, an employer must try to accommodate you.

The most frequent exercise of this right arises with a person with a disability. The company's obligation to accommodate does not apply to persons with medical conditions unless the medical conditions rise to the level of a disability, and the courts have sometimes been restrictive in the interpretation of what constitutes a disability.

For employees, the good news is that these rights are favored in the law and employers who deny accommodations are required to prove that the suggested accommodation—an equipment modification, for example—imposes an "undue hardship" on the company.

In a sense, the "undue hardship" defense discriminates against larger employers. In failure-to-accommodate situations, larger employers with more extensive resources at their disposal are expected to do more than smaller entities.

Tip: If you need an accommodation, submit a written request to your HR department or supervisor, along with any supporting medical documentation or other evidence. Always add something to the effect of, "If this accommodation does not work, I am open to other reasonable accommodations and am available to discuss other options you prefer."

Unlawful Interference

As with pass interference in football, an employer will draw a flag if it interferes with your exercise of certain protected rights.

This type of situation arises most often regarding your right to unpaid medical leave under the Family and Medical Leave Act. The most common form of FMLA claim involves retaliation for *using* FMLA leave; interference comes about when your company discourages you from using FMLA or denies you the right to use FMLA.

There are less common and more difficult types of interference, such as interference with your right to retirement benefits or another type of employee benefit under a company plan.

Tip: Always document your efforts to seek rights to which you believe you are entitled. For example, if you are absent from work for medical reasons and your employer decides not to recognize your absence as covered by the FMLA, obtain copies of your medical information related to your absence and put your request for FMLA leave in writing.

Unlawful Disparate Impact Discrimination

The least common form of unlawful discrimination arises in the context of company requirements that have a statistically disparate, or disproportionate, impact on a protected class. Such policies are only legal if the requirement is a "bona fide occupational qualification."

A classic example of unlawful disparate impact arose within the airline industry in the 1960s because of the airlines' desire to have female "stewardesses" on flights. The airlines wanted young, beautiful, and unmarried stewardesses to appeal to their businessmen customers. The definition went so far as to require female flight attendants to resign when they turned 35 or if they got married. This requirement obviously excluded male and older applicants. The airlines defended the policy by citing surveys of their customers' preference for young, female stewardesses. Needless to say, the airlines lost, and we now have "flight attendants."

Disparate impact claims also arise with respect to public safety employees, such as police officers and firefighters, since some municipalities require that employees be under a certain age. In those situations, municipalities have often been successful by arguing that certain physical abilities are a "business necessity."

Tip: If your employer has a policy or practice that excludes all or a disproportionate number of members of a protected class, examine whether the policy is necessary for the operation of the business. For example, if your company requires you to engage in some type of physical performance test, determine whether the required results (lifting 50 pounds) are really necessary to do the particular job. These types of claims are particularly complicated and, in recent years, fewer such cases have been filed because most employers no longer have such policies.

Part 4

Understanding Your Rights as a Job Applicant

Do I Have Any Rights When I Apply for a Job?

When you are a job applicant, the anti-discrimination laws passed by Congress and your state legislature generally apply. In addition to protecting you from unlawful biases while you are employed or if you are fired or laid off, these laws are applicable during the hiring process.

A prospective employer who is subject to these laws cannot discriminate against you on the basis of race, color, sex, age, national origin, religion, or other protected characteristics. For this reason, employers are not supposed to ask questions during the pre-hire process that would reveal any of your protected statuses. Obviously, your name will likely reveal your gender, but that is an exception.

The most common form of discrimination that occurs during the hiring process is age discrimination. For this reason, it is generally advisable not to include information on a resumé that would enable an employer to guess your age. If you list college graduation dates or employment dates 20 or more years ago on your resumé, for example, it is fairly obvious that you are at least 40 years old.

What Should and Shouldn't I Put on My Resumé?

Resumés or curriculum vitae are often critical when seeking a job that does not require completion of an application form. Resumés must be carefully drafted. They should be designed to attract the recipient's interest by focusing on your career goals and your relevant accomplishments.

The two biggest sins with respect to the substance of resumés concern 1) a failure to explain a recent termination, and 2) the desire to tell your entire life's story.

The first sin is a sin of omission most often seen with employees who are simply the victims of workforce reductions or layoffs. Most employees include a description of their most recent job on a resumé, but fail to explain why they are looking for a job.

Your resumé is a great opportunity to remove any suspicions if you are in a circumstance where your termination is explainable. Consequently, if you have been terminated by an employer unrelated to any performance or conduct issues, explain the facts on your resumé. Similarly, if you quit a job for some legitimate personal reason, include that information on your resumé.

Including an explanation as to why you are looking for a job may give you a leg up on your competition, because many other applicants will only disclose that they are currently unemployed and looking for a job, creating a measure of doubt in the potential employer's mind.

The second sin that occurs frequently on resumés is the seemingly universal temptation to tell your entire life story and career history on the resumé. Instead, you should limit information about your career to a relevant period of time, perhaps no more than the most recent 10 years. Although you might have been a wonderful employee 20 to 30 years ago, your performance that long ago is likely of little or no interest to a prospective employer, particularly in certain rapidly changing industries. It is more important to highlight and emphasize what you have done lately.

Indeed, when older applicants tell their life history, they are unwittingly telling prospective employers their age. A person who lists a 30- or 40-year-career on a resumé is hardly hiding the fact that he or she is 50 or 60 years old. If you are an older applicant looking for employment, you should always remember that the most common form of employment discrimination is discrimination against older job applicants. A resumé should never reveal that an applicant is more than 40 years of age or so. As previously noted, dates of graduation from high school or college reveal information about your age, or at least create assumptions about your age. The important thing you need to convey is your educational level, not when you received your degree or diploma.

Given this advice, a common response is, "Well, won't they figure out my age when they interview me?" The answer is likely "yes" unless you don't look your age, but the key is getting an interview in the first place. If your resumé is appealing enough to warrant an interview, then you have the opportunity to sell yourself in person and alleviate potential reservations about your age.

Tip: Depending on the breadth of jobs you are seeking, you may wish to make multiple versions of your resumé so you can highlight different skills with different employers. If you do, however, keep track of which potential employers received which version!

What Should I Say if I Am Asked Why I Left My Last Job?

This is one of the most difficult questions facing job applicants who have lost one or more of their most recent jobs involuntarily. In short, honesty is the best policy. Applicants should be careful to accurately describe the circumstances about any separation, and provide any relevant explanation.

If you lost your last job for economic reasons, such as a layoff or reduction in force, make sure your prospective employer knows that. In that instance, you should not reflect your job loss as a "termination"; instead, describe it for what it was: a separation without cause due to business conditions. In response to a "reason for leaving" question, state something like, "Although I was meeting expectations, the company had a layoff and I was one of the newest employees at the company" [or "I was one of the newest employees in my department.]."

If you quit your job, explain that the decision was voluntary, such as, "I resigned from that job because I wanted to search full time for a better job that makes full use of my skills and abilities."

Tip 1: If you were terminated from a previous employer for misconduct or unsatisfactory work performance, be sure to include an explanation that is as favorable to you as possible. Include in your explanation what you learned from the experience. For example, you might say, "In my last job, I cared a lot about the quality of my work and invested the necessary time and attention to do it right. As such, I was not able to work fast enough to meet the production target set for me. I am looking for a job where my attention to detail will be an asset."

Tip 2: If you are terminated, have a clear understanding of what your former employer will say to a prospective employer. Will they call it a resignation, a termination, or a job elimination, or will they simply confirm dates of employment?

What Can My Former Employer Say to a Prospective Employer?

Prospective employers who are considering an applicant for employment often check references, including the most recent employer and previous employers.

Beginning in the 1970s, many employers began a practice of not providing negative references to prospective employers out of fear of being sued for defamation by a former employee. Basically, a practice developed whereby former employers would only confirm dates of employment, last position held, and sometimes salary information.

The result of this common practice was a belief by many individuals that employers were legally prohibited from providing anything but the most basic information. Nothing could be further from the truth. Former employers are generally permitted to state facts or express opinions about a former employee. Thus, "Blinn was fired for absenteeism" is permissible so long as it is factually accurate, i.e., that Blinn was either absent excessively or the company believed she was absent excessively.

Any limitation upon the right of a former employer to provide information about an employee is governed by state law. The law varies to some extent from state to state, but many states allow former employers to provide employment references with no liability for defamation unless the former employee can demonstrate that the information was provided maliciously. Without such a statute, a former employee need only demonstrate that the employer provided false information and that the providing of the false information resulted in the failure to obtain a job.

In states that grant this protection, commonly called a "qualified privilege," it is next to impossible for an applicant to take any legal action against a former employer who provides information about his or her employment.

Upon separation from employment, and particularly if there is a severance proposal presented to an employee, it is critical that an employee obtain an agreement from the former employer as to the type of information that will be released to any third party. It is common in severance agreements for an employer to assert a provision that the employee will not criticize or disparage the former employer; a former employee needs to insist that such a provision is mutual and that the employer will not provide any negative information about the individual's employment.

An employee who fails to reach an understanding with a former employer about the information that will be provided to a prospective employer has very limited recourse in the event that false information is provided by a former employer. This is one of several non-economic terms of separation that should be considered when evaluating any severance proposal provided by an employer. Employees frequently focus simply on the amount of severance without appropriate focus on non-economic matters that could haunt them for years to come.

Tip: *If you leave a company and severance negotiation does not take place, you should still determine what your former company will say about you to prospective employers. Ideally you should obtain a letter of reference from your supervisor that will paint you in a positive light. Lacking that, it is still beneficial to obtain a letter indicating that the company does not provide information about former employees beyond dates of employment. That way, when your former employer does not come forth with a positive recommendation about you, it will not be construed as "damning with faint praise."*

Can a Prospective Employer Ask Questions That Will Reveal My Age, Race, or Medical Problems?

Job applicants completing an employment application should be careful to complete it as accurately and truthfully as possible. Incorrect information on an employment application may disqualify an applicant from consideration for employment. False information can even be used later by an employer as a reason for discharge if the employer was not aware of the false information at the time of the application.

Today, federal and state laws and regulations prohibit employers from soliciting information in employment applications that is not considered relevant in employment decisions. Only what are known as "bona fide occupational qualifications" (BFOQ) may be used as criteria in determining whether an applicant can effectively perform a given job. Obvious characteristics that must be excluded from consideration are the age, race, gender, or religious affiliation of applicants unless any of those characteristics is essential in doing a job. One example of permissible discrimination would be allowing the manufacturer of women's clothing to hire only female models for a fashion show featuring its products.

For employers that are large enough to be covered by the Americans with Disabilities Act, it is also unlawful to inquire about an applicant's health status until a conditional offer of employment has been made. Only then may an employer inquire into physical or mental conditions that may limit an applicant's ability to perform the job or jobs in question.

Tip: If you are completing a job application that requests information that should not be considered, the best course is to complete the application nonetheless and maintain a copy for your records. If you are not hired after completing the application, you should consider contacting an employment lawyer or the Equal Employment Opportunity Commission.

Should I Sign a Non-Compete Agreement When I Am Hired?

This area is particularly tricky. Some employers routinely require new hires to sign documents that restrict their right to compete if they leave the company regardless of whether their departure is voluntary or involuntary. Your bargaining power is limited in these situations, but you should make sure you understand the agreements before signing them.

Enforcement of restrictive agreements is a matter of each state's laws, and it is wise to check with an employment lawyer to understand the likelihood that such an agreement could be enforced in the future. In California, most non-competes are void as a matter of state law, but California is unique in this regard.

Tip: Once you understand the non-compete agreement you are being asked to sign, it might be possible to negotiate less restrictive terms, such as reducing the period of the restriction or making the agreement apply only if you are terminated with just cause or if you resign. An ideal non-compete agreement includes a provision for payment of severance for the length of the non-compete in the event that you are fired without just cause or if you resign with good cause (so-called "garden leave" agreements). In these instances, you should carefully review how the company defines just cause or good cause.

Should I Worry About the Non-Compete Agreement I Signed with My Last Employer?

A prior non-compete is something to be concerned about if your new job will potentially require you to violate its terms. Non-competes are generally enforceable in most states (except California) to the extent they are reasonable in scope. If you ignore a prior restriction, you may subject yourself and your new company to a lawsuit to enforce its terms.

Whether any previous employer will try to enforce the agreement often depends upon how much of a threat you pose to its business interests.

Tip: *If you have a non-compete agreement, make sure you provide a prospective employer with a copy of the agreement if a new job may be in violation of the non-compete. If your former employer believes you are violating the agreement and wants to enforce it, both you and your new employer will likely be notified of the company's intention. You do not want your new employer to be surprised and learn of your prior non-compete agreement in this manner.*

What Documents Should I Sign When I Am Hired?

There are various documents that you should sign upon employment. The specific documents will vary by employer, but these include tax withholding documents, an I-9 form to verify your immigration status, and a health insurance application if health insurance is offered to you. Be sure to understand how much it will cost you for health insurance and how much your employer will contribute, if anything.

Tip: *Be sure you claim the proper number of dependents for your tax situation so an appropriate amount can be withheld from your paycheck.*

Is an Employment Offer a Contract?

According to established contract principles, a contract is formed if one party makes an offer and the other party accepts it. Such contracts may be evidenced by writings (an offer letter), e-mail exchanges, and even verbal offers. With the latter, it is advisable to confirm the terms of any offer that you accept by sending an e-mail or other written communication to the person making the verbal offer.

If you accept an offer of employment, make sure the essential terms are documented, such as your pay and benefits, any agreement as to a term of employment, and representations as to any conditions for continued employment.

Tip: Maintain hard copies of all documents and e-mail between you and your prospective employer about the terms and conditions of your new job.

When Should I Get Legal Advice Before Accepting a Job?

Normally, you do not need legal advice before accepting a job. However, if you are presented with any type of restrictive agreement (non-competes and non-solicitation agreements), it is advisable to consult employment counsel in your state to understand the ramifications of such agreements and your ability to negotiate the terms.

It is often advisable to seek a legal opinion if you are asked to sign a formal employment contract for the same reasons. Too often, new employees merely sign these documents only to be surprised later when and if they leave their job.

Tip: You will not offend most prospective employers by obtaining legal advice about the meaning of any documents you are being asked to sign before accepting a job. If they are offended or do not allow an appropriate amount of time for review of the documents, beware!

Part 5

Understanding Your Rights as an Employee

What Rights Do I Have on the Job?

There are many misconceptions in the workplace that flow from an underlying belief that, in addition to rights protecting you from unlawful discrimination, you have a right to fair treatment and respect on the job. Part 5 of this book addresses subjects that often arise during tenure of employment regarding employee rights.

Most of the answers to questions about employee rights are based on two principles: 1) Your duty of loyalty to your employer, and your freedom to leave; and 2) Your company's right to run its business as it sees fit unless there is a law that restricts it.

Which Laws Protect Me?

As noted earlier, a plethora of federal and state laws exist today that provide protection against discrimination, unsafe working conditions, and retaliation. Other laws govern your rights to minimum pay and overtime, your rights in the event of an illness or injury, and your right to "blow the whistle." These laws are summarized in Parts 7 and 8.

Tip: You should have a basic understanding of your rights so you avoid making mistakes that could haunt you later. Too often, employees come to lawyers after their termination only to discover that they did something based on a misunderstanding of their rights that turns out later to hurt their case.

Do Independent Contractors Have the Same Rights as Employees?

With very limited exceptions, independent contractors are not covered by employment discrimination or retaliation laws. The reason is simple: Independent contractors are not employees, and these laws generally protect employees. There are some limited exceptions, with the primary ones being state or federal whistleblower laws that protect persons (not just employees) who report fraud, illegal conduct, or other improper activities.

Even if you are called an independent contractor, it is possible that you are actually an employee. Some employers attempt to limit benefits that they pay for employees by designating certain individuals as independent contractors when in fact the contractors are treated like employees. In general, you are an employee if your employer has the right to control the manner and means of your work performance.

Do I Have an Employment Contract?

It is often thought that only professional athletes, top executives, and certain white-collar professionals have a "contract of employment." While it is true that many athletes and executives have written employment contracts, often in conjunction with inflated salaries, it is also true that every employee has an employment contract of one form or another.

A contract of employment can be oral or written, and it is simply an agreement between an employer and employee as to certain conditions of employment. Every employee has at least an oral contract as to compensation for the work that he or she will perform for an employer. If an employer agrees to hire a person to perform work for a company, a contract is formed as to the person's compensation, whether it is compensation by the hour or on a salaried basis.

Simply put, every employee has some kind of agreement with his or her employer. Although formal, written agreements generally cover many more aspects of the employment relationships than do informal ones, it is simply incorrect to state, "I do not have an employment contract with my employer."

Tip: If a person who is accepting employment is in a position to negotiate, it is often advisable to expand the agreement to include such things as job security, severance pay in the event of termination without cause, and future compensation arrangements. While most employees are not in a position to negotiate limitations on an employer's right to control those aspects of employment in the future, individuals should take advantage of whatever opportunities they have to negotiate such terms in advance of employment.

I Am Employed by a Public Employer; Do I Have Different Rights Than if I Worked for a Private Company?

This book is intended to provide information about the rights and responsibilities of employees in the private, non-union workforce. Occasional references are made to unionized employees and to non-private, or public, employment situations, but considerations for employees in those settings often differ from those affecting the private workforce.

Public employees should be aware that, generally, they have greater employment and job security rights than employees in the private sector. Such employees should make sure they are knowledgeable about their rights.

To the extent that public employees have greater job security than private employees, many state laws require employees to exercise such rights within a very short period of time. Consequently, if you are a public employee, you should know your rights prior to an adverse action by your employer so that you will be able to take timely steps to protect your interests.

Public employees can learn their rights either by asking for information from their employer's human resources department, by researching the issues on the Internet, or by consulting with an experienced employment attorney who is familiar with the rights and responsibilities of public employees.

Tip: As with any employment situation, employees should consult a specialist familiar with employment law rather than a general practitioner who may not be current on public employment law. Local bar associations can usually provide assistance in finding an attorney in virtually any area of law, including public employment law.

Do I Have More Rights if I Am Covered by a Union Contract?

Yes. Union contracts generally provide the greatest job security of all—the right to be protected from discipline or discharge unless the company has "just cause." Just cause is much broader than the protection afforded by federal and state laws against discrimination or retaliation, because those laws require you to prove some unlawful motive. Just cause usually includes the idea of being free from discrimination or retaliation (by definition, unlawful discrimination or retaliation does not comport with the definition of just cause), but it also requires the company to actually prove a good reason for its action.

It is the limitation on management's discretion to make personnel decisions that motivates most employers to fight union organizing attempts. Most union contracts limit so-called "management rights."

Union contracts often provide greater rights in the areas of layoffs, promotional opportunities, and employee benefits than exist in non-union settings.

If you are covered by a union contract, you also have a right to "fair representation" by the union even if you are not a member of the union. This duty of the union is lower than the malpractice standard imposed on doctors and lawyers, but it does prohibit your union from acting arbitrarily or capriciously.

Tip: *Regardless of your opinion of your union or any union representatives, it is best to "bite your tongue" because you might need their help some day!*

When Am I Entitled to Overtime Pay?

Under the Fair Labor Standards Act and comparable state laws, you are entitled to overtime pay if you are 1) a non-exempt employee, and 2) you work more than 40 hours in a particular workweek. Overtime laws are among the most frequently violated laws and often result in employers being charged with "class action" violations.

If you are an hourly wage worker, you are "non-exempt." If you are a salaried worker, do not automatically assume that you are "exempt" or that you are not entitled to overtime. See "The Fair Labor Standards Act" in Part 7 for a fuller description of the legal requirements to be considered an exempt employee.

In determining whether you worked more than 40 hours in a given week, you may include all the time that your employer required you to be present at work. For example, under a 2005 Supreme Court decision, workers in a beef processing plant were entitled to be paid for the time spent traveling between the "donning and doffing" changing area (where they dressed in required protective clothing) and the workers' assigned locations on the production line.

If you have a pressing concern about overtime pay, there are employment lawyers around the U.S. who specialize in overtime cases. Likewise, the United States Department of Labor's Wage and Hour Division enforces overtime laws.

Tip 1: If you work more than 40 hours in a week, keep a record of your time, particularly if your employer does not maintain detailed accounting of your time or simply puts "40 hours" on your paycheck. Your records may be very persuasive to either the Department of Labor or a court if your employer does not keep an accurate time system and you are entitled to overtime compensation.

Tip 2: Wage and hour laws are complicated, and it is particularly important to make sure that the employment lawyer with whom you consult has experience in this subject area and in your state.

Am I Entitled to Pay During a Medical Leave of Absence?

You are only entitled to pay during a medical leave of absence if your employer's policies provide for such pay, such as through a short-term or long-term disability policy, or if you have accrued vacation or sick pay at the time of your leave of absence.

The Family and Medical Leave Act (FMLA) protects your job for up to twelve weeks if you are eligible for that law's coverage, but it does not require that you be paid. Many employers' FMLA policies require you to use any short-term disability pay and any accrued vacation or sick pay during any FMLA–covered leave.

Only employers with at least 50 employees are covered by the FMLA, but some states have enacted analogous laws for smaller employers.

Many employers violate the FMLA by failing to recognize absences as FMLA–covered absences. Absences covered by the FMLA cannot be used against you under company attendance plans. This law is highly litigated.

Tip: If you are covered by the FMLA or a similar state law, always advise your employer if a leave of absence is caused by a serious medical condition, regardless of the duration of the leave. The act provides protection against retaliation for taking FMLA leave as long as your employer has enough information to know that your absence is covered by the FMLA.

Can My Employer Discipline or Fire Me for Being Absent from Work if I Have a Medical Excuse?

Unless you are protected by the Family and Medical Leave Act or an analogous state law, employers in most states can lawfully discipline or fire you from being absent from work even if your absence is caused by a medical condition. Of course, your employer cannot discriminate against you by treating you differently than other employees with similar absences, and your employer must honor the Americans with Disabilities Act.

The good news is that most employers do not discipline employees for a limited number of "excused" absences, and most absences for medical reasons are excused. Your company is permitted to require medical documentation of your absence, and to require a medical release for you to return to work.

Am I Entitled to Receive Either Short-Term or Long-Term Disability if I Have Been Disabled?

Short-term disability pay is usually limited to a period of either 13 or 26 weeks. Long-term disability pay typically extends up to two years or age 65. Both types of coverage are available to you only if your employer provides such coverage automatically, or if you elect to participate in a plan that requires some contribution from you. Employers are not required to provide either kind of disability benefit.

If your employer does not provide a disability pay benefit, or if the benefit offered is not sufficient in your estimation, you may purchase a private disability policy through an insurance company. As with life insurance, the premium for a disability policy is less expensive for younger employees.

Understanding any policy's definition of "disabled" is important. For example, most short-term policies require only that you be disabled from your current job; some long-term disability policies only pay a benefit if you are totally disabled from most or all jobs. If you decide to purchase a private disability policy, shop around not only for the best price, but also the most lenient definition of "disability."

Tip: Particularly if you receive long-term disability pay, the employer or insurance company will carefully monitor your continuing eligibility. If you have a problem obtaining benefits or have other problems while on disability leave, a federal law called ERISA (see Part 7) may be applicable. Be aware that relatively few lawyers specialize in this area and you should make sure your lawyer is qualified.

What Are My Rights to Vacation and Other Paid Time Off?

You have no "right" to paid vacation or other paid time off unless your employer provides the benefit as part of your compensation.

If your employer provides such a benefit, it is basically a matter of contract law. Thus, you are entitled to use it based upon the agreement with, or promise by, the company. Often, employers outline the rules for such use in an employee handbook or similar writing.

One common question concerns the issue of carrying over unused paid time off to a succeeding year. Again, this is governed solely by your company's agreement or policy. Some employers say "use it or lose it"; others allow carry-over to a succeeding year or years, but with a limit on how much can be accrued.

Tip: *It is a good practice to take a real vacation, without being chained to your computer or cell phone. Speak with your boss about how your duties— including responses to voicemail and e-mail— will be handled while you are away so that you do not feel compelled to work while on vacation. You owe it to your mental health to take a periodic break.*

What Should I Do if I Am Injured on the Job?

Workers' compensation laws in all states provide pay (based on your average weekly wage) and medical benefits if you are injured on the job. Consequently, you should always give your employer notice of any workplace injury, and you should ask whether the injury affects your employment status. In most states, it is illegal to retaliate against an employee for making a workers' compensation claim.

Generally, so long as your injury occurs "in the course and scope" of your job, you will be entitled to compensation for days missed from work and for related medical bills. A common issue that arises is whether an injury occurred at work or was simply an aggravation of some non–work-related condition.

Another frequent sticking point concerns traveling to and from work versus going from one worksite to another. Generally, getting to and from work is not covered by workers' compensation laws, but traveling within the work day for a job-related purpose is covered. However, workers' compensation laws vary from state to state and legal advice might be necessary if your employer disputes your claim.

Being paid after being injured at work and having your medical expenses reimbursed is the good news about workers' compensation. The bad news is that workers' compensation laws offer only limited benefits (a percentage of your weekly wages), and you generally lose the option of filing a personal injury claim for other damages that you would have been able to pursue if the same accident occurred outside of work.

Workplace injuries also raise other issues, such as whether you are protected by the Family and Medical Leave Act, are eligible for short- or long-term disability benefits, and/or are protected by the Americans with Disabilities Act or other analogous state laws.

Tip: Always maintain copies of disability and life insurance benefit plans that your employer offers. For serious injuries, consider consulting with a lawyer in your state.

Does My Company Have to Follow Its Employee Handbook?

Employee handbooks have become the norm in American workplaces. Back in the day, work rules were often simply tacked to a wall in the factory, locker room, or lunchroom. Today, statements of work rules have evolved into more formal documents, ranging from several pages to several hundreds of pages.

Most employee handbooks create no "rights" for employees, and often contain a disclaimer of any legal significance. Most handbooks today contain language that goes something like this: "This handbook is intended merely to state current company policies and practices. It does not create or imply any obligation on the part of the company to follow these policies or practices, and the company specifically reserves the right to change, alter, amend, or ignore these policies at any time, with or without notice to employees."

Despite such blanket disclaimers, employee handbooks are valuable documents for employees to read and understand. Most employers attempt to follow their handbook and, in some circumstances, employers can be convinced to alter a particular course of conduct based upon language in a company handbook.

Unfortunately, employee handbooks are regularly distributed, but seldom read. For new employees, a review of the employee handbook often reveals much about how an employer treats its employees. Handbooks are generally written with the best of intentions and, the more detailed and specific a handbook is with respect to an employer's policies, the more likely it is that an employer will act in accordance with its policies.

In addition, many employee handbooks, while not legal documents, explain the legal rights and responsibilities of employees. For example, most employees are unfamiliar with the benefits afforded by the Family and Medical Leave Act, which provides for up to 12 weeks of unpaid leave in the event of a serious illness for the employee or a close family member. While the nature and duration of leaves authorized by the FMLA are standard across all eligible employers, the manner in which the FMLA is implemented can and does vary across employers.

Tip: *Employee handbooks contain valuable information for employees who believe they have been treated wrongfully during their employment or as a result of a termination. You should always keep a copy on hand in case you need to refer to it. In general, an employer who applies its policies inconsistently is more likely to open itself up to a successful claim of employment discrimination. Knowing what the employer says it would do in a particular instance is important information in the event that you are subjected to adverse treatment.*

Which Laws Apply When the Company is Making Promotion Decisions?

All federal and state laws that ban discrimination and/or retaliation in the workplace apply to promotion decisions, just as they do to hiring decisions. In some ways, claims of biased promotion decisions are easier to prove than termination decisions, because it is possible to identify the person or persons who were preferred.

If you feel that you have been unfairly passed over for a promotion, first identify the candidate who was awarded the job. Then, determine if that candidate belongs to a different protected class or, in the instance of a younger candidate, whether the person is substantially younger than you, i.e., at least 7 to 8 years younger.

If your work record and qualifications are objectively superior to those of the successful candidate, it may be worth investigating a potential claim. The difficulty arises from the fact that you, as a current employee, may not want to rock the boat while still employed, and your financial losses may not be sufficient to justify the time and expense associated with making a legal claim.

Tip 1: Before complaining to Human Resources or speaking with a lawyer or governmental agency, ask for an explanation from the decision maker as to why you were not selected. Document what you are told and try to objectively evaluate whether the reasons are valid.

Tip 2: You are not married to your employer. If you are passed over for a promotion that you deserved, it might be a good time to dust off your resumé and begin a discreet job search.

Am I Entitled to Receive a Performance Review?

Performance reviews, while something most employees like to have, are not legally required. Many employees who are terminated after several years of employment without receiving any performance reviews believe that performance reviews are mandatory for their employer. This is simply not the case.

Regular performance reviews are a recommended practice in virtually every employment setting. When done correctly, performance reviews can benefit both the employer and the employee.

Employers are regularly advised by their legal counsel to conduct performance reviews, with an emphasis on doing them regularly and fairly. Too often, performance reviews are done hurriedly and are not seen as a high priority. In addition, many supervisors are reluctant to provide honest feedback. The best performance reviews acknowledge satisfactory (or exceptional) performance and provide constructive feedback.

When performance reviews are given to employees, it is certainly fair and reasonable for an employee to provide his or her reaction to the performance review. In fact, many formal performance review documents provide space in which an employee can make comments.

It is a good practice for employees to request and keep copies of performance reviews. Employers are not legally obligated to provide a copy of a performance review to an employee, but it never hurts to ask.

Tip: Regardless of whether an employee can record comments directly on the performance review, an employee who disagrees with a particular review should always consider submitting a written response to the employer. Any such communication should be composed in a professional manner, noting the specific areas of disagreement and citing examples to substantiate your positions. The more specific the rebuttal, the better. General comments such as, "I do not agree with this review," are of little benefit to the employer and do not carry much weight in the event of subsequent wrongful discharge litigation.

Am I Entitled to Receive Warnings?

Many employers have established disciplinary systems that provide for warnings when employees' performance falls below acceptable standards or when they violate work rules. These systems have become so commonplace that many individuals believe employers are legally required to provide warnings prior to making a decision to terminate an employee. It is not uncommon for employment lawyers to hear comments such as the following:

- "I have a great case. I worked for the company for seven years and was fired without a warning."
- "I came to work every day and did exactly what was expected of me. No one ever complained about my performance, and then one day, I was fired. I never saw it coming."

With the caveat that existing employment discrimination laws might apply when an employee receives no warning prior to discharge, employers in non-unionized workforces are not legally required to provide any type of warning to an employee prior to termination. If that is an employee's only complaint about how he or she was treated by an employer, the failure to provide any advance warning before termination will likely be of no consequence.

On the other hand, collective bargaining agreements between unionized employers and a union representing employees generally provide that employees should receive progressive discipline prior to termination. In unionized workplaces, the failure to provide any previous warning may be grounds to challenge a termination through the grievance and arbitration process contained in the applicable collective bargaining agreement.

Even when an employer has a policy or collective bargaining agreement that requires prior warnings, warnings are almost never required in the case of serious misconduct within the workplace. Still, employment discrimination laws might provide some relief if other employees have been treated differently than the terminated employee.

Tip: As with performance reviews, always request a copy of any disciplinary warning, and prepare a well-reasoned, written rebuttal if you disagree with either the facts or the level of discipline. A written rebuttal is advisable even if the warning is verbal.

Should I Sign Warnings or Performance Reviews?

Many employees who receive performance reviews or disciplinary notices with which they disagree are fearful that signing these documents will imply they agree with them. Absent specific language on the documents to that effect, such a concern is misplaced.

Today, most disciplinary documents make it clear that a signature by the employee only means that he or she has read and/or received a copy of the document. Many documents of this nature contain specific language such as, "By signing, you acknowledge receipt of this document."

If a performance review or disciplinary warning requires an employee's signature but does not contain explanatory language as to the meaning of the signature, it is advisable for the employee to sign the document but add a statement to the effect of, "My signature means only that I have reviewed and/or received a copy of this document."

As previously mentioned, it is also advisable to write a rebuttal to any document that an employee receives concerning work performance or discipline with which the employee disagrees. In such an instance, an employee should request that the company place a copy of the rebuttal either as an attachment to the document in question or as a separate document to be maintained in the employee's personnel file.

Tip: As with other important documents, it is wise to request a copy of any performance review or discipline that is documented by your employer. Keep such documents in a file outside of the workplace, because you can never be sure that you will have an opportunity to retrieve documents from your workplace in the event of a termination.

What Should I Do if I Receive Unfair Discipline or an Unfair Performance Review?

If you receive what you believe to be unfair discipline or an unfair performance review, you should discuss it with your supervisor, and document in a clear, professional manner all the reasons why you believe were treated unfairly. If you are in a unionized workplace, consult with a union steward about the possibility of filing a grievance.

When employers formally address performance concerns, they are often trying to improve your performance by emphasizing the seriousness of their concerns, but they are also creating a paper trail to support a later decision to terminate your employment.

You are wise to make sure that your disagreement is likewise put in writing so that your supervisor, as well as the human resources department, is on notice about your concerns. After creating your documentation, request that it be made a part of your personnel file.

Always address your rebuttal about unfair action to a particular person (ideally an HR representative or a supervisor), and include your name and the date. While you are within your rights to request a response within a reasonable amount of time, the key is to submit your documentation in a timely fashion.

Tip: If you feel that your job is in jeopardy based upon some action by your employer that you believe to be unfair, such as a "final warning," it might be appropriate to obtain advice from an employment lawyer. Too many employees wait until after a discharge to understand their rights in the workplace.

What Should I Do if My Boss Is a Jerk But He's Not Violating Any Laws?

Many an employment lawyer has heard this kind of refrain from a potential client: "That place was terrible. My boss treated all of us horribly. He was always harassing us about everything and he had no respect for our feelings or our opinion. I want to sue him and the company for all the trouble they put me through."

An employee's worst nightmare is a bad boss. Bad bosses can make life miserable for even the best employees by showing no regard for employees' desire to be treated with dignity and respect.

Unfortunately, existing employment laws do not make it illegal to be a harassing, disrespectful, "bad" boss. In fact, "equal opportunity harassers" have more legal protection than bosses who harass individuals selectively.

Harassment on the job is only illegal in most jurisdictions if the harassment is conducted in a discriminatory fashion of some sort, with the classic example being sexual harassment. In rare circumstances, individuals in other protected classes may also be able to claim illegal harassment if it can be demonstrated that the particular boss directed his harassment at, for example, older or disabled workers.

When faced with a situation of an equal opportunity harasser, employees should be proactive in complaining about the harassment to appropriate company officials. Most employers have anti-harassment policies that extend beyond illegal forms of harassment. Any complaint submitted to an employer claiming that a boss is harassing employees should be as specific as possible and, preferably, be submitted by more than one employee. The more employees who complain about a particular supervisor's bad behavior, the more likely an employer is to do something about the situation.

Beyond dealing with harassing behavior, experience indicates that the best, but often most difficult, way to handle the "jerk" boss is through group action, whereby employees band together and present an internal complaint about the boss to Human Resources or a higher ranking company official. Although it can be intimidating to step forward, it is best that these complaints not be made anonymously so that management can conduct an appropriate investigation.

Tip 1: Many bad bosses exhibit bullying behavior and, once they learn of one or more such complaints, will back off. In these instances, standing up to bullying behavior can be very effective. Nonetheless, there is always some measure of risk of retaliation by the boss, who may learn or guess the identity of the complainers even though that information is not made known. Group action is important because the National Labor Relations Act (summarized in Part 7), protects from retaliation even non-union employees who engage in "concerted activity." Concerted activity is conduct undertaken by employees on behalf of two or more employees. If you complain only about how you yourself were treated, that complaint is not protected.

*   **Tip 2:** *If you work for a jerk and suspect he will remain with the company, it may be a good time to begin a job search. Too many employees remain stubbornly loyal to a company that tolerates a jerk. There are many other options for you and your career, and it is always easier to find a job while you have a job.*

When Does Harassment Become Illegal?

Unlawful sexual or racial harassment—the most common forms of unlawful harassment—or harassment based on another protected characteristic such as age, national origin, disability, or religion, are all forms of unlawful discrimination prohibited by various federal and state laws.

In general, unlawful harassment comes in two varieties. "Quid pro quo" harassment occurs when favorable treatment of some sort—job advancement, a pay raise, or maintaining your job—is conditioned on succumbing to an *unwelcomed* advance. These claims most often arise either when a worker faces retaliation after refusing a sexual advance or after terminating a previously consensual relationship.

The second type of unlawful harassment is the "hostile environment." Remember, a hostile environment is not in itself illegal, as many bosses or workplaces are hostile in some sense. Only environments that are hostile based on a protected characteristic are unlawful.

Moreover, isolated hostility such as a one-time racial or ethnic slur that is based on a protected characteristic is usually not unlawful. Instead, the courts have made it clear that harassment of this type must be "severe and pervasive" from the standpoint of a reasonable person in order for it to be deemed beyond legal bounds.

What Should I Do if I Am Being Harassed by a Co-Worker?

If you are being subjected to unlawful harassment on the job, such as sexual or racial harassment, it is critical to distinguish between harassment by a co-worker and harassment by a supervisor. If you are being unlawfully harassed by a co-worker, the U.S. Supreme Court has ruled very clearly that an employer has no liability if it was not made aware of the unlawful conduct and given an opportunity to correct it.

For this reason, most employers have a written policy advising employees to make a complaint to an appropriate company official—usually specified in the policy—so that the company may investigate. If you are in such a situation, review the policy carefully and document the alleged harassment clearly so that you can make as specific a complaint as possible.

If an employer responds to a complaint of co-worker harassment with "prompt, effective" action, the employer will generally be shielded from liability. You must first give the company the opportunity to correct the problem caused by one or more co-workers before you can maintain a successful legal claim based on unlawful co-worker harassment.

Be aware that although companies often state that they will conduct a confidential investigation, it is often difficult for them to do so.

Tip: Not all co-worker "harassment" is unlawful. Nonetheless, management should be aware of any type of substantial or persistent harassment. Every employee deserves to be protected from unwanted or unsavory treatment by a co-worker. Although you risk possible retaliation by the harasser when you make such a complaint, the laws against retaliation do provide protection for employees who make good faith complaints of unlawful harassment.

What Should I Do if I Am Being Harassed by a Supervisor?

As discussed on the previous page, employers are not liable for unreported harassment by a co-worker. In contrast, employers are liable for unlawful harassment by a company supervisor. Thus, you may make a legal claim about such harassment even if you have not filed a formal complaint with the company.

The classic example of unlawful supervisory harassment is a boss who makes unwelcomed sexual advances toward a subordinate. It is often difficult for an employee to complain out of fear of retaliation by the boss.

Nonetheless, the preferred course is first to make it very clear to the boss that the advances are unwelcomed.

- "I appreciate your interest in me, but I am happily married and I am not interested in any type of relationship with you beyond our working relationship."
- "I am uncomfortable with you making comments of a sexual nature to me and ask you to stop so I can focus on doing my job."

As with other advice about problems encountered by employees, it is best to either put the message in writing—an e-mail, for example—or otherwise contemporaneously document the message.

Tip: If the unwelcomed harassment continues, consulting with someone you trust in Human Resources or higher management is still a good idea before making a formal complaint. If the harassment is severe and you do not feel comfortable discussing the matter internally, it makes sense to consult an experienced employment attorney who represents employees.

What Can I Do About the "He Said/She Said" Problem?

The "he said/she said" problem arises when people believe that third party witnesses are required before deciding whether to believe one person or another. Frankly, this is ridiculous when you think about how you make decisions every day as to the believability of information that you read or hear.

It is not uncommon to hear in the workplace, "Well, we can't do anything because it's his word against her word." All too often this is a refrain from a human resources investigator regarding a complaint of racial or sexual harassment. This type of comment is either disingenuous or is simply an excuse to avoid making a hard decision about who is more likely telling the truth. Can you ever imagine an employer saying, "Joan said she saw Doug steal $50 from petty cash, but Doug denied it, so we can't do anything."? Employers have an obligation to establish, to the best of their ability, the veracity of the parties involved and the strength of the evidence at hand.

Tip: If your employer dismisses your complaint of harassment because there are no corroborating witnesses, explain very clearly why you are telling the truth and provide any documents that you have, such as notes you've taken. You will be well within bounds to insist upon a resolution of who is telling the truth.

Is a "Performance Improvement Plan" a Sign of Trouble?

Yes. Performance Improvement Plans, or "PIPs," have come into vogue as the last step in an employee's discipline progression before termination. Employers often use PIPs to show that they tried everything to help an employee before deciding to terminate the worker. The action plans in PIPs are often difficult for an employee to satisfy.

PIPs usually identify "challenges" or "opportunities" for the employee to overcome, as well as specific goals to correct the deficiencies. They often last 30 to 90 days. It is common for them to contain a statement that failure to meet PIP expectations may result in termination.

If you are placed on a PIP, you should be on guard and make sure you document any unrealistic expectations ("I cannot achieve this goal because...."), or point out any areas of disagreement at the time the PIP is given to you. You should also document your progress and successes during the PIP, and note any failure of your boss during the PIP ("My boss said he would meet with me every two weeks during my 90-day PIP, but we only had one meeting.").

Tip 1: In the event that you suspect you are being unfairly criticized or singled out, this may be a good time to gather information on co-workers who are not being treated in a manner similar to you. You should record information such as name, position, length of service, any known performance issues, and/or protected class membership.

Tip 2: If ever you were to consider advice from an employment lawyer, receipt of a PIP is a good time to do so.

What Should I Do if I Suspect My Job Is in Jeopardy?

We are all familiar with the growing trend of employers documenting an employee's poor work performance or disciplinary history. In response to rising employment litigation, lawyers representing companies have advised their clients that they need "a paper trail" in order to protect themselves in wrongful discharge litigation.

Supervisors and other leaders within organizations are constantly reminded to document counselings, warnings, and other events in the workplace that may impact an employee's job security.

By the same token, employees—particularly those who fear that their job may be in jeopardy—need to create a paper trail of their own, or as some say, "document your employer." As important as keeping a job is in today's economy, maintaining a diary of sorts of your employment involves a minimal investment of time that can prove invaluable if you are disciplined or terminated.

Documentation of your employer should include positive remarks or writings about your contributions, a general description of unrecognized job accomplishments, and observation of the employer's conduct in the workplace toward you and other employees like you.

In addition, if you sense that you are being treated differently than another employee outside one of the protected classes, you should document those observations as well.

Tip: This type of diary should be maintained away from the workplace, either in paper form (such as a notebook) or on a personal computer. Never leave such diaries or notes on company property because there is a risk that they will be lost, found by someone else, or inaccessible in the event of termination.

A diary of this sort helps to counterbalance the impact of any paper trail that your employer creates in order to justify an unfair termination.

What Should I Do if My Employer Offers a Voluntary Separation Program?

"Voluntary" separation programs are sometimes offered by employers in an effort to reduce a workforce without—or before—initiating an involuntary workforce reduction. Most voluntary plans offer employees some severance pay and other benefits in exchange for the worker's agreement to resign.

If truly voluntary, the plans can be a wonderful benefit for employees who are willing to move on for personal reasons, whether to make a desired career change or because of dissatisfaction with their current job or employer. Still others take advantage of the opportunity to facilitate an early retirement.

Unfortunately, some employers and bosses use this kind of opportunity to pressure some employees to leave, making remarks such as, "If you don't take this package, you should be aware that we have concerns about your performance."

Deciding whether to take a voluntary package should be carefully considered. The following "decision tree" analysis may be helpful.

The first question to ask yourself is, "Do I think offering it to me and not to others in similar positions is unfair?" If that answer is "no," then the decision is simply whether you want to leave or not, and then you accept or decline the package accordingly.

If the answer to the first question is "yes," then the second question is, "Do I want to leave by the time my employer wants me to leave?" If the answer is "no," then consider negotiating the end date to accommodate how long you would like to stay or how long you think it might take to find a suitable job.

If the answer to both questions is "yes," then whether you negotiate involves weighing whether burning some bridges will be worth the effort to achieve a modest improvement in the offer. Many employers will not negotiate the terms of voluntary offers unless you retain counsel to negotiate on your behalf.

Tip: Litigation rarely if ever makes sense over any offer of a voluntary package, so leverage in negotiations is low. The only exception is when there is serious "arm twisting" to get you to take a package and you refuse, and then the company terminates you soon afterward. In that event your leverage might be greater because you have been terminated, and you may have legitimate legal claims based on the unfairness.

What if I Am Called to a Meeting and Suspect I Am Being Fired?

Many employees who believe that their job may be in jeopardy are suddenly given notice of a meeting that will take place within minutes or hours, and they suspect it will result in the termination of their employment. With such short notice, it is often difficult to obtain legal advice regarding one's rights in the particular situation.

If you are called to such a meeting and do not have sufficient time to obtain legal advice, you should document as soon as possible what was said to you during the meeting, and request copies of any documents that the employer relied on in making its decision to let you go. Once a termination decision is made, employers will rarely reverse such decisions based upon anything that you say in such a meeting beyond your explanation of the facts relied upon by the employer. Thus, it is generally wise to remember the old adage, "You have two ears and one mouth." Most importantly, you should listen as carefully as possible during such a meeting, and then consider whether you should contact an employment attorney to review your concerns.

Tip: As with other matters, documentation is critical. Your memory as to events that may have taken place several days or weeks before will fade, and you should record as quickly as possible the reasons that you are given for any particular adverse action.

Do I Have a Right to Privacy at Work?

The right to privacy is recognized in most states, and an employer may not invade certain private interests such as family, medical, sexual, or other very personal matters. Most states, however, offer no protection against many seemingly private matters, such as your off-duty conduct, or your use of e-mail or the Internet for personal matters at work. Only some states will offer relief for employees who feel that their legitimate expectations of privacy have been violated absent a showing of some business need.

The U.S. Constitution protects public sector employees to a greater degree than private sector employees because the Fourth Amendment prohibits unreasonable searches and seizures by local, state, and federal government agencies. For example, most public sector employees, unlike private sector employees, are protected against random drug testing.

Tip: *Do not do anything that would expose you to possible discipline or disapproval by your employer, even if your behavior occurs off-duty. In general, you have a duty of loyalty to your employer and, unless your activity is recognized as protected by some law, you likely have no relief if your employer objects to your conduct.*

Can My Company Search "My" Locker or Other Property on Company Premises?

Nothing infuriates employees more than an invasion of privacy by a supervisor or other official searching a locker, a computer, or even bodily fluids by way of a drug or alcohol test. Many employees believe that, while they are in private employment, state or federal constitutions protect their privacy in the workplace. This is a wrong assumption.

Simply put, when you, as an employee, enter the private property of your employer, you generally leave any constitutional rights to privacy at the front door. There are exceptions for certain private employers who do business with state or federal governments, but the only restriction on most searches in a private workplace are rooted in concepts of common sense and human decency unless you can establish some legitimate expectation of privacy.

Whether it is your locker, your desk, or the company's computer that you use in connection with your work, never assume that a supervisor is not able to inspect such areas. As such, it is usually advisable not to access private e-mail accounts on a company's computer, because most private employers have the right to inspect those computers and can monitor your e-mail or track websites you have visited.

If you would be embarrassed by something that is in your locker, desk, or work computer, it should be removed. Remember that "deleting" e-mails from a computer does not necessarily mean that the e-mails are gone; forensic specialists can usually retrieve e-mail and other computer information long after the computer user thinks that he or she has deleted it.

Tip: Treat the employer's premises as you would your front yard. Don't allow anything to be on the property that would subject you to embarrassment or unwanted scrutiny.

Am I Entitled to Review "My" Personnel File?

Employees often refer to the personnel file maintained by the company as "my personnel file." To be sure, the file maintained by the employer is about you, but it is certainly not your file.

For employees engaged in work for a private employer, there is a common misperception that an employee has some legal right to review the personnel file. Nothing could be further from the truth. The file is the property of the employer and the employer may decide whether to allow an employee to review such a file or not. (If you maintain a diary of your employment, you would certainly agree that the company has *no right* to review that diary even though the diary may be about the company.)

On the other hand, in most, if not all, jurisdictions, state public record laws require that public employee records, including personnel files, be available to the public. In those circumstances, an employee has a legal right to review the file since any member of the public may also review that file.

Although the employee's personnel file in private employment settings is company property, it is fair for an employee to periodically ask to review the file to ensure that information contained within the file is accurate. While not legally required to do so, many employers grant such access. Moreover, it is also fair for an employee to prepare "rebuttal" documents in response to any negative material contained within the file, and to ask the employer to place the rebuttal document in the file. Again, there is no legal requirement that the employer keep the material in the file, but many employers will voluntarily do so.

Can My Employer Monitor My Computer Usage at Work?

Unless you have a union contract or some other contract that protects your right to use your computer at work for personal matters, most states allow an employer to monitor your computer usage, and many employers do just that. Only California, Connecticut, and Delaware have taken any action in this area to limit an employer's ability to monitor your usage.

Federal law provides some protection against monitoring your use of private e-mail or tracking your personal logon information and password on a non-work Internet service providers' server. Employers may, however, monitor e-mail stored on your work computer or associated with your work e-mail address.

It is nearly impossible to delete anything you do on your computer. Pressing the delete button will not completely destroy a communication since IT specialists can readily see what you have deleted and track which sites you have visited.

You should avoid maintaining personal information, such as financial records, on your work computer unless you have no problem with your employer having access to that information.

Tip: E-mail is often so important in employment and other litigation that some trial attorneys call it "evidence mail" instead of electronic mail. If you are a supervisor, be mindful that your e-mail messages about employees can be easily obtained during the discovery phase of litigation.

Can My Employer Monitor My Personal Calls at Work?

Under federal law, companies can only monitor personal phone calls with your consent, and employers are only permitted to monitor business calls. If your employer monitors a business call but realizes that the call is personal, it must cease monitoring the conversation.

Some states grant broader protection by requiring both you and the other party to provide consent before monitoring can begin. However, these limitations do not change the fact that your employer may lawfully bar you from making any personal calls at work or limit the number or duration of calls, so long as the rule applies equally to other similarly situated employees.

Tip: If you are concerned about whether your employer is monitoring your personal calls, use your cell phone or some other phone for your personal discussions.

Can My Employer Require Me to Take a Polygraph (Lie Detector) Test?

With very limited exception, your employer cannot require you to submit to a polygraph test (known to most people as a "lie detector"). In 1988, Congress passed The Employee Polygraph Protection Act, and it applies to almost all employees and job applicants. See Part 7 for a more complete description of the act.

Can My Employer Require Me to Disclose My Social Media Passwords?

The answer to this question is "maybe." As this book went to press, much controversy had been created by a limited number of employers demanding access to Facebook and other social media accounts by requiring disclosure of passwords. State and federal legislators have threatened to take action to ban such requirements.

Tip: If your employer requests or demands your social media passwords and you are concerned about your privacy and/or the content that could be seen, consult with a computer expert about ways to remove inappropriate content prior to providing access, or as soon as possible thereafter.

May I Audiotape Conversations at Work?

In most states and under current federal law, you may audiotape conversations at work unless your employer has a rule or policy against doing so. Some states require that each party to the conversation consent to the audiotaping.

Sometimes employees believe they should audiotape conversations to obtain evidence that will protect them in the future. Their reasons for doing so can include anticipating a wrongful discharge, or suspecting that a harasser will deny having made certain remarks. Be forewarned, however, that some judges and jurors look with disfavor upon audiotapes that are conducted secretly. You may be just as well off by immediately documenting a conversation or an event after its conclusion. If you do so, date the document and, if possible, have a witness sign the document as having been prepared on that date.

Tip: Much like employers are advised to document unsatisfactory performance of an employee, you should document unsatisfactory performance by your supervisor or another company official. What's good for the goose is good for the gander!

Can My Employer Subject Me to a Drug Test?

Yes. All employees are subject to drug testing. However, many states require an employer to have "reasonable suspicion" before drug testing an employee. Most states, however, do not have such a requirement for employees in the private sector.

If you test positive, an employer should treat you in a manner similar to the way it has treated other employees who have tested positive.

Tip: *If you are drug tested and receive a positive result that you believe should have been negative, it may be prudent to obtain an independent test as soon as possible. An independent drug screen days later may offer little protection against a false positive.*

Can My Employer Enforce a Dress Code?

Yes, provided the dress code applies to all similarly situated employees. For example, a dress code for one gender but not the other would violate state and/or federal laws prohibiting sex discrimination. A company may have one dress code for females and one for men, so long as neither sex has a greater burden in complying with the requirement.

Can My Employer Implement a "No Smokers" and/or a "No Smoking" Policy?

More than half of the states make it illegal for employers to invoke any disciplinary or discriminatory action against employees who smoke outside of work hours and off the employer's property. Legal off-duty behavior such as smoking, while perhaps not desirable to some employers from a health insurance standpoint, cannot be prohibited in these states. In states without this protective legislation, however, your employer may invoke a requirement that you not smoke at all, and may reinforce this requirement through mandatory nicotine testing.

A few states with "smokers' rights" legislation make it permissible for employers to offer health, disability, and life insurance coverage at different rates for smokers and non-smokers, but the varying rates must be based on actual costs incurred by employers or on actuarial projections.

If you reside in a state without "smokers' rights" legislation, employers are within their rights to exclude smokers when evaluating job applicants. Most do not do so, however, for reasons of equity and narrowing of the talent pool. Many employers instead focus their efforts on offering smoking cessation programs for their employees.

In contrast to decisions on hiring and discipline relative to smoking, employers have much more latitude in deciding whether or not to permit smoking on their property. This holds true even if their company is located in a "smokers' rights" state. Where not already prohibited by law (some states prohibit smoking in every workplace, whether public or private), employers may choose to enact any manner of smoking restrictions of their own for employees or visitors on company property.

Can I Blog or Post Facebook Comments About Work Issues on My Own Time?

If you have a blog, Twitter account, or social media page and discuss work-related matters in these media, be careful. Many employers have policies that may apply to your activity, such as rules requiring you to protect the company's reputation and maintain the secrecy of confidential information.

Bottom line: If your employer learns that you disclosed information it deems harmful, it will be difficult for you to challenge any discipline unless you had authority from your employer in advance of publication, which is unlikely. Another exception might be if you know that your employer has not taken disciplinary action against other employees after being made aware of similar behavior.

Tip: If you are dying to vent about your employer on your blog, either restrict access to your blog or blog anonymously. Better yet, talk to a trusted friend or family member!

Can I Moonlight?

"Moonlighting" is the term for having a second or third job to supplement the income from your primary occupation. In general, you are permitted to moonlight unless you have signed an employment agreement to devote all of your working time to a single employer.

Despite this general rule, there are limits to moonlighting that arise out of your common law "duty of loyalty" to each employer. Thus, you should not moonlight for a competitor of your other employer(s), and you should not work where you would be required (or able) to divulge confidential information of an employer.

Tip: It is often wise to disclose a second job to your first employer. Disclosure can help in the event of any work schedule issues that arise, and may even lead to a discussion about the adequacy of your pay. However, you may still face a conflict if one job's schedule conflicts with your other job, and no employer has an obligation to accommodate your other job's work schedule.

What Should I Do If I'm Just Unhappy on the Job?

If you are unhappy in your job, feel free to look for another one. You are a free agent! Never count on the legal system to guarantee you a favorable outcome even if you are convinced you are being treated unlawfully in your current job.

Too many employees who are unhappy in their current workplace fail to begin any sort of job search while they are still employed. Instead, they complain to their family, co-workers, and friends about the lousy workplace, somehow imagining that the work environment will change in magical fashion.

Loyalty is a two-way street. While it is admirable for you to be loyal to your current employer, it makes little sense to be loyal if that loyalty is not returned in kind. Nothing requires any employee to remain with an employer. After all, involuntary servitude was outlawed by the Thirteenth Amendment in 1864!

Today, it is relatively easy to conduct job searches outside of the work day by responding to opportunities posted on the Internet, as well as those in more traditional media such as newspapers and industry trade magazines. If you are currently employed, your cover letter should advise a prospective employer that you are employed and that your inquiry should be treated in total confidence. Be sure a prospective employer knows to contact you somewhere other than at your work address.

Even if you are perfectly happy in your job, you should always be aware of alternative employment opportunities that might help you achieve your career goals. You owe it to yourself and your family! There is little risk involved in looking, and it doesn't make sense to miss a potentially fantastic opportunity because of complacency in your current position.

Tip: Having said that, few things bother an employer more than learning a current employee is looking for another job. Regardless of the circumstances in any individual workplace, supervisors often expect current employees to remain loyal to the company as if the company is being "generous" by providing a job. Never make it known that you are looking for another job while you are still employed.

How Good Are Internal Complaint Procedures?

Many employers have established internal grievance procedures, even in workplaces that are non-union. These procedures usually allow an employee to submit a complaint to Human Resources or to the company's personnel department. Some larger companies have set up an ombudsman's office that is distinct from HR and is charged with reviewing a whole host of issues that arise within a company, job-related or otherwise.

These procedures are sometimes a good way to document your concerns and place your employer on notice that you disagree with treatment you have received. While initiating a grievance is often the right thing to do, there is no guarantee of success, since HR may rely on a supervisor's version of events, or may not have the time or resources to truly investigate the issue fully.

Nonetheless, these procedures are useful in ensuring that there is a record of your concerns in the company's files. Too many employees who receive unfair treatment simply don't put their concerns in writing, resulting in a file that contains only a supervisor's opinion or version of events.

Grievance procedures sometimes allow former employees to challenge a termination decision. If you believe your termination was unlawful, it is wise to consult with counsel before making your complaint so you can accurately record facts and circumstances in a manner that does not later impact a potential legal claim. Be aware that these processes commonly have a short deadline, so act quickly in seeking counsel if you wish to file a grievance.

Tip: If you are not able to obtain legal advice in time to meet your company's deadline to file a complaint, include a statement as follows: "I will supplement this complaint with further information as soon as possible."

Am I Required to Complain Internally Before Making a Legal Claim?

With limited exceptions, you are not required to complain internally before making a legal claim.

The clearest exception is in the instance of unlawful co-worker harassment, discussed previously. If you are being harassed by one or more coworkers, you are generally required to place your company on notice of the harassment so that your employer has an opportunity to address the issue before you file a legal claim.

Another exception arises if your company has established a mandatory alternative dispute resolution program, discussed next.

Tip: If you are considering a legal claim, check with an employment lawyer to determine whether you first have to exhaust any internal procedures.

What Are "Alternative Dispute Resolution" Programs, and Do They Affect My Right to Go to Court?

Alternative dispute resolution (ADR) programs are becoming more prevalent all the time. If properly formulated, these plans allow your employer to require you, as a condition of employment or continuing employment, to agree to arbitrate any claim outside of court in a private procedure decided by a qualified arbitrator.

To be lawful, these plans must allow you to bring any claim that you could pursue in court before an arbitrator, and they must include procedures that allow you to prepare for a hearing in much the same way you would if you were involved in a lawsuit. For example, an arbitration program cannot require you to pay a filing fee or any other fee in excess of fees you would incur with a lawsuit.

Employers often tout arbitration as a faster, more efficient manner of resolving disputes. The truth is that they are only faster and more efficient if you allow your company to move the case too quickly, thus denying you the opportunity to gather the necessary information that your attorney could discover in a lawsuit.

The other truth of these "ADR" programs is that your company wants to avoid the possibility of a jury trial. Almost all employers would prefer that a judge or arbitrator decide a case, fearing that the working people who typically comprise juries are likely to be sympathetic to an employee's complaint.

Tip: Treat your obligation to go through a mandatory arbitration program the same as you would a lawsuit. Don't accept the idea that somehow you don't need a lawyer. You are still pursuing a legal claim, and you need legal representation.

Should I Trust Human Resources?

Human resources professionals are often in a most difficult spot: they sincerely want to help employees with problems on the job, but they receive their paychecks from the company with which employees are at issue. In addition, they receive much of their information from company supervisors who have a vested interest in making sure their decisions are supported by HR.

Human Resources is often a valuable source of information about employee benefits, company policies, and applicable rules promulgated by the employer. An HR representative can usually be relied upon for that type of information, and for obtaining any documentation you might need.

On the other hand, you cannot always count on HR to fairly evaluate workplace disputes. The reasons include the natural tension between wanting to stand up for employees in the face of unfair treatment and knowing that HR's decisions must also be received favorably by the company. In addition, HR professionals often do not have the time and authority to examine all the relevant facts, particularly when they are faced with claims of possible discrimination.

In most situations, the best you can do is make a clear complaint to HR, making sure that your supporting information is well documented. You can generally trust that your information will be presented to appropriate supervisors, and that your documentation will be preserved.

Always remember that some legal claims, such as harassment by a co-worker, require you to bring the complaint to the attention of management or you will lose your right to file a successful legal claim. Then, regardless of how the complaint is resolved internally, you may go outside the organization and seek a legal remedy.

Should I Trust My Union?

Unions and their representatives have a legal obligation to fairly represent employees within any particular bargaining unit. They are given great leeway by the courts, however, and only in very extreme cases will they incur any liability for failure to adequately represent a member.

One problem encountered in union representation is when one member has an interest conflicting with one or more other members. In these situations, unions are often disinclined to favor one of its members over another (e.g., when you challenge another employee being promoted ahead of you).

Another common problem is that unions have limited financial resources and do not process all meritorious discharge cases to arbitration because of the legal fees and expenses required to do so. Unfortunately, union lawyers do not prosecute those cases on a contingency fee–basis, and unions tend not to arbitrate the most difficult or risky cases.

Finally, union representatives are often not schooled in the intricacies of employment discrimination. Thus, they tend to focus on whether "just cause" exists for an employer's disciplinary decisions rather than whether other similarly situated employees have been treated in a similar manner.

Tip: Although not perfect, your union is your best friend in resolving workplace issues because 1) representation is paid for through your union dues, and 2) whether "just cause" exists is usually easier to prove than a claim under one of the many federal statutes. Understand that your representative has many different matters to handle, so you must be patient in waiting for your concern to be addressed. Keep in mind that if you believe your union is violating its duty of fair representation, you have only six months to file a charge with the National Labor Relations Board.

Should I Seek Legal Counsel Before I Am Fired?

Consulting with an employment attorney is advisable if you believe termination of your employment is on the horizon and you believe that you have been treated unlawfully.

Many employment lawyers will advise you concerning your rights in the workplace while you are still employed, but you should expect to pay for the advice. Some lawyers will charge a nominal fee for lower income employees but, even if they don't, spending a few hundred dollars for advice to protect your job is usually worth it. Without any advice, you may lose a job you may have been able to protect, or you may not take necessary steps to help you in a later legal claim.

Always remember that you should consult with a lawyer who is experienced in representing employees. All too often, employees ask a lawyer they know for advice without knowing whether the attorney has sufficient experience representing employees.

Tip: Obtaining a referral from another lawyer is always a good idea, as most lawyers are either familiar with local lawyers who represent employees or know where to direct you.

Can I File A Lawsuit if I Have Problems on the Job But I Am Not Fired?

Many employees who suffer discrimination in the workplace are victimized by illegal treatment but are in a catch-22: Do I put up with the discrimination to keep my job, or do I take legal action to protect my rights? This is a difficult question and requires a critical analysis of your job security, how you are being affected by the illegal discrimination, and your ability to survive if you are then a victim of retaliation.

As a practical matter, filing a lawsuit is difficult for any current employee because economic losses are the driving force behind settlements and verdicts. Thus, if you suffer discrimination on the job but have not suffered significant financial losses, it is usually not affordable to engage in litigation with your current employer. Even though attorneys' fees may be awarded if you prove your case in court, most employment discrimination lawyers are reluctant to engage in lengthy litigation because attorneys' fees and costs are only recoverable if you achieve a court victory. Although legal fees may be a factor in settlement discussions, the reality is that most employers will not settle employment discrimination claims of a current employee by agreeing to pay significant legal bills if the discrimination did not cause the employee significant financial losses.

Tip: *If you are being discriminated against on the job, you should carefully document the facts and circumstances that you believe support your claim. Some companies allow employees the opportunity to file internal grievances or complaints, but it is wise to consult with an experienced employment lawyer to determine whether such a complaint is worth the effort.*

Part 6

Understanding Your Rights
If You Are Fired

Am I Entitled to Unemployment Compensation?

You are generally entitled to unemployment compensation unless you have voluntarily resigned, committed some type of misconduct, or engaged in other behavior that would constitute "just cause" under your particular state's law. The eligibility standards for unemployment compensation vary from state to state.

If you are unsure whether you qualify for unemployment compensation, the best way to find out is to apply for it. If you do not qualify, the state will tell you why and you can evaluate whether the state's reasons are accurate.

Remember that only "voluntary" resignations disqualify you from unemployment compensation. If you feel that you were forced to quit because your working conditions were not tolerable, or your employer allowed you to resign in lieu of termination, apply for unemployment and explain the circumstances under which you felt compelled to quit.

Tip: Employers are charged a small premium for unemployment insurance. A single claim will usually have little or no impact on that premium, so many employers do not challenge unemployment claims even if they think you do not qualify.

If I Believe I Have a Legal Claim Against My Former Employer, Should I Find a Job, or Will That Hurt My Chances of Collecting Money?

Even if you think you have a strong legal claim against your former employer, you have a legal duty to mitigate your losses by looking for comparable work and, after a reasonable amount of time, looking for something less comparable.

It's true that a new job will lower the damages that you could collect by way of settlement or a court victory, since net lost wages are the most common form of damages. But it's also true that you have a 100% chance of getting paid from a job. You never have a 100% chance of collecting money by suing your former employer.

Am I Bound by the Non-Compete Agreement I Signed?

Most restrictive covenants, including non-competition and non-solicitation agreements, apply even if you are fired from your job. Rarely, an agreement will state that it only applies if you quit or are fired with just cause.

Many employees who have signed non-compete agreements wrongly believe that restrictions only apply if they quit, even though the agreements usually stipulate that they apply if you separate from employment "for any reason."

Remember, non-compete agreements are governed by state law, and there are broad differences from state to state. For example, as stated previously, California deems almost all non-compete agreements unenforceable (even if you work in California for an employer based in another state and your employer claims the agreement is governed by another state's laws), whereas Kentucky takes a strong stand in favor of enforcing them. Many states have laws or court decisions that allow enforcement of non-competes to the extent that the agreements are reasonable.

Tip: If you find yourself in a situation where you have lost a job, have signed a non-compete, and want to work for a competitor, find an employment lawyer with experience litigating non-compete cases. This is a specialized area of employment law. Sometimes it makes sense to obtain a written legal opinion as to whether, and how, a non-compete can be enforced in order to provide the opinion to a prospective employer.

Do I Have a Right to Receive My Accrued Vacation or Other Paid Time Off if I Quit or Am Fired?

Many employees wrongly believe that accrued vacation or other paid time off has already been "earned" and thus they are legally entitled to it upon separation from an employer.

In general, you have no "legal" right to accrued vacation or other paid time off if you leave your employment for whatever reason. Whether you are entitled to receive such an accrual depends on your company's policy. It is essentially a matter of contract. Most employers will not provide accrued pay if you quit or are fired for what the company believes is "just cause."

Tip: If you anticipate quitting or being terminated, review your employer's policies on payment of accrued paid time off. You can sometimes make use of the benefit before leaving, or negotiate for it as part of a severance agreement.

Am I Entitled to COBRA Continued Medical Coverage?

You are entitled to continuing group medical coverage under COBRA (the Consolidated Omnibus Budget Reconciliation Act) if your former employer has at least 20 employees and you lost your job for something other than "gross misconduct."

In addition to federal coverage afforded by COBRA, many states have COBRA-type laws, which you can learn about by calling your state's insurance department.

Tip: *In the very rare event that your former employer denies you COBRA coverage because of alleged gross misconduct, you should negotiate to have that allegation removed from your record. COBRA costs your employer nothing except your continued claim experience—good or bad—and your employer may agree to change its characterization of your dismissal to simple misconduct, particularly if your claim history is not likely to increase the group's insurance costs.*

Can My Employer Enforce Restrictive Covenants?

We live in a capitalistic society that promotes the idea of competition and the ability of individuals to pursue the occupation of their choice. As a consequence, many employees wrongly believe that somehow restrictive covenants should not apply to them because, "I have a right to make a living."

The term "restrictive covenant" refers to agreements between an employer and an employee that limit the employee's post-employment activities. If you have signed one, be careful.

The restrictive covenant most widely known is the non-competition agreement that more employers are requiring employees to sign as a condition of being hired or as a condition of continued employment. Non-competition agreements generally preclude employees from accepting work with a competitor after their employment with the original company terminates. The duration of the restriction varies, but often ranges from 6 to 24 months.

Restrictive covenants also include limitations on use of a company's confidential information following a separation from the employer. These agreements are often coupled with non-competition provisions in the same document.

Another example of a restrictive covenant is a "non-solicitation" provision that limits an employee's ability to solicit customers and/or employees following the termination of his or her employment. These provisions are normally limited in duration, again commonly somewhere between 6 months and 2 years.

Whether any particular restrictive covenant is enforceable is dependent upon state law rather than federal law. As mentioned previously, California is unique in deeming most non-competes void as a matter of law; the Commonwealth of Kentucky strongly favors the enforcement of non-competition agreements, and such agreements are generally enforced as written.

One principal problem with restrictive covenants is that they are often required of new employees, and new employees are loathe to refuse to sign such documents at the beginning of their employment. All employees who are asked to sign non-competition or non-solicitation agreements should at least understand the potential future impact of those agreements before the documents are signed. It is advisable to seek a legal opinion as to the anticipated enforcement of any such document so that you can then make a reasoned decision about whether to sign or not.

Tip: It is possible to negotiate the terms of restrictive covenants when they are presented to an employee. Common subjects of negotiation include the duration of the agreement and whether the employer will pay severance of any sort during the term of the restrictive covenant.

Employees who obtain legal advice on the enforcement of such covenants are in a better position to negotiate the terms of the covenants with a prospective employer.

The bottom line: Do not assume that a restrictive covenant is not enforceable post-employment simply because, "I have a right to feed my family."

Am I Entitled to Severance?

"Severance pay" is compensation paid to an employee following a separation of employment. Generally, severance pay is provided to employees in recognition of past service and to assist them during the time of transition between one job and another.

Absent an agreement between an employer and employee, there is generally no legal right to severance pay. Many companies have adopted severance pay policies and put them in print, but even these are subject to change without notice from the employer.

Generally, severance pay is more common among larger employers who provide such pay to employees separated from employment "without cause." In almost every line of work, severance pay is not provided to employees who are terminated "for cause" or voluntarily resign from their employment.

The amount of severance pay provided varies considerably, although one common rule of thumb is that severance will range from one week per year of service to one month per year of service, depending upon the particular job involved. Lower level employees are closer to the one week per year of service standard.

Lower paying positions are easier to fill because the supply of lower paying jobs is greater than the supply of higher-level jobs. Logically, an employee earning $10.00 per hour should be able to gain comparable employment in a shorter period of time than someone earning $30.00 per hour.

Tip: Any employee who is terminated without cause should consider negotiating for severance pay, and possibly seek the help of legal counsel, particularly if a job search is expected to be prolonged.

Severance pay policies that limit employees' ability to collect such compensation only for the duration of their unemployment are becoming more common. For example, one company provides severance pay of two weeks per year of service, but specifically states that it will discontinue severance pay if the separated employee obtains other employment.

Such policies serve as a disincentive for a terminated employee to gain other employment early in the severance pay period. You should consider negotiating with your employer to remove this disincentive by emphasizing that an important principle of severance pay is that it is intended as a reward for accumulated service to the employer.

What Should I Expect In a Severance Agreement?

Severance agreements serve two general purposes: 1) As noted previously, you receive compensation to recognize your past service and assist in your transition to new employment, and 2) Your former employer receives a "release of claims" to guarantee that you will not take legal action in the future related to your past employment.

Once you sign such an agreement, it is almost always fully enforceable, even if you later discover facts that would help you in a legal claim. If you believe you have potential legal claims, consult with an employment lawyer first so that you understand whether your severance amount is a fair exchange for your legal claims.

Most severance agreements specify the dollar amount of severance, whether you will receive any other pay (for example, accrued sick or vacation pay), and provisions for continuation of benefits during the severance period. Your agreement should also state your rights to continued health insurance through COBRA if you are eligible for such coverage as a result of being in a group plan.

In addition, your employer will typically include a lengthy description of the claims you are releasing (even though a simple "you release all claims whatsoever" would probably do), a confidentiality clause to limit whom you can tell about the agreement, a "non-disparagement" clause limiting your right to criticize your company, and a "no-rehire" provision.

Severance agreements will also state whether your separation is a resignation, a termination, or a result of something else (a reorganization or reduction in force, for example). If your employer characterizes your termination as a resignation, whether it was made voluntarily or by the employer offering you the opportunity, make sure it is clear that you still qualify for unemployment compensation. Just because you agree to quit in lieu of being terminated does not mean that you have voluntarily quit.

Most agreements will also include a provision for maintaining the confidentiality of any trade secrets or other proprietary information you have gained during your employment. Sometimes, an employer will try to slip in a new non-compete agreement or other restrictive covenant.

If you are 40 years of age or older, the severance agreement should also include language required by the Older Workers Benefit Protection Act (OWBPA). This law requires the company to advise you of your right to consult with a lawyer, allows you at least 21 days to consider accepting the agreement (45 days if you are part of a group of employees being let go), and establishes your right to revoke the agreement within 7 days of signing if you change your mind. See Part 7 for a fuller description of your OWBPA rights.

Tip: Severance agreements seem very one-sided because much of the language appears to favor the company. This is almost always the case, but most of the language is not a big deal provided the amount of severance is fair. As the saying goes, "You get the money, they get the language."

How Can I Get a Better Severance Offer?

Severance agreements are often open to discussion. Treat the first offer made to you as a starting point. You can either negotiate with your company yourself, particularly if you remain on good terms, or you can retain an employment lawyer to do so on your behalf.

Many employers will negotiate certain additional terms to a severance offer as a matter of course. These should include whether the company will oppose unemployment compensation, whether it will give you a letter of reference, and what the company will say about you to a prospective employer. These are non-economic terms that are generally negotiable.

Occasionally, an employer will adjust the amount of severance if you press for a better offer, but expect only modest monetary improvements, if any, when you negotiate without a lawyer. Companies are sometimes willing to pay for outplacement assistance as part of a severance arrangement. Although outplacement services don't add to your bank account as would more severance, they can be instrumental in helping you find a good job sooner so you can begin earning a paycheck again.

If you believe you have been treated unlawfully and the severance is not sufficient, or the agreement includes new terms that restrict your future employment, hire an employment lawyer to negotiate on your behalf. Some employment lawyers will charge you an hourly fee, and others will charge you only if they are able to increase the financial terms of the deal.

Tip: A severance agreement is a legal document, so consult with an attorney if you do not fully understand its terms. A given agreement might not protect your best interests even though the severance amount seems fair.

What Should I Do if I Am in a Union and I Am Fired?

If you are in a union or are covered by a collective bargaining agreement (even if you do not belong to the union), direct your union to file a grievance IMMEDIATELY if you believe your termination was without just cause. In most collective bargaining agreements, there is a short period of time to file a grievance, and if you miss it, you lose your right to grieve.

Once your union files a grievance, cooperate fully with your union representative and provide him or her with all the information related to your termination. Many employees are not patient enough with their unions and fail to respect the fact that their representatives have a number of other matters to address. Remember that in grieving your discharge, your union representative is your best friend. He or she will be responsible for negotiating on your behalf.

If you believe your union is not representing you fairly, do not "jump the gun" and file an unfair labor practice against your union for failing to honor its duty of fair representation. Work with your representative to resolve any conflicts.

Unions are held to a lower standard of representation than a lawyer, and they fail that standard only if their representation is arbitrary, discriminatory, or capricious. In general, mistakes do not rise to the level of a viable charge.

Tip: *Filing a charge with the National Labor Relations Board alleging your union has violated its duty of fair representation should be a last resort. If it comes to that, however, remember that you only have six months to file such a charge.*

Are Headhunters and Outplacement Professionals Any Good?

Headhunters, or persons whose job it is to find new employees for companies, can be a valuable asset in your job search, particularly for higher-level positions. Headhunters generally seek out qualified candidates who are working at other companies, or evaluate resumés of job-hunters who have sought them out. They are paid by the companies who contract with them to find qualified candidates for certain positions.

If you are seeking a higher-level position, find local headhunters or "executive search firms" and notify them of your availability. They will often request a resumé, a list of references, and any other information you can provide about your qualifications in a particular line of work.

Outplacement firms are companies that are hired by employers to assist displaced workers in finding a new job. They are often retained during reductions in force or layoffs that impact a large number of individuals. Typically, their services are offered as part of a severance package.

The best outplacement firms provide help with resumés and applications, offer training on how to secure and succeed in interviews, share information about available positions in your area or industry, help you build your contact network, and sometimes provide clerical assistance and an office setting for your use.

When you are out of work, finding a job should be your full-time job, and headhunters and outplacement professionals can help.

Are There Government Agencies That Will Help Me if I Am Fired?

There are many state and federal government agencies that can assist you if you lose your job. States have unemployment offices for purposes of administering unemployment compensation, and many provide job seekers with information about available jobs within a community. In addition, state insurance departments can provide information about health insurance and related benefits.

The primary agencies of the federal government that can assist you are the U.S. Equal Employment Opportunity Commission, the United States Department of Labor, and (for unionized workers) the National Labor Relations Board. These agencies investigate potential claims of unlawful treatment, but there are usually strict time limits within which to make a claim or inquiry.

Some potential legal claims, such as claims of discrimination under federal law, require you to first file a charge with the government agency. See Part 7 for information on the time limits and whether an initial resort to a government agency is required before filing a lawsuit.

Each state also has comparable agencies to investigate charges of discrimination, pay issues, and the like.

Governmental agencies often do not have the resources or manpower of a law firm to fully investigate a claim. Thus, do not be discouraged if an agency dismisses your claim or if you feel that your claim has not been fully investigated. Instead, request a copy of the agency's file under the Freedom of Information Act and seek legal help in evaluating the finding. Be aware of time limits that may be applicable to filing a legal claim once an agency closes its investigation, because they are usually short and strictly enforced.

Tip: If you plan to contact a government agency for assistance, at least consider consulting with an employment lawyer before filing anything. Employees, being unfamiliar with employment law, can unwittingly say things to a governmental agent that will undermine their eventual claim.

Do I Have Any Obligations to a Former Employer?

Your obligation to a former employer is generally governed by state law. In most states, you are obligated to maintain the confidentiality of trade secrets that you have obtained during your employment.

In addition, as previously discussed, you are sometimes bound by agreements you have signed with your former employer that may go well beyond state law, such as promises you made in a severance agreement or in restrictive covenants.

Tip: As a general rule, it is not a good idea to speak critically of your former employer. You never know how word travels among people in your industry, and you don't want to burn any bridges that you could need in the future. Some things in life just don't work out as we would like them to; taking the high road is a good rule of thumb.

Part 7

Federal Law Exceptions to
Employment at Will

Does Federal Employment Law Apply to Me?

In the United States, the most comprehensive legislation protecting you as an employee has been enacted by Congress on the federal level. These laws are exceptions to the employment-at-will doctrine discussed extensively in Part 1.

The following pages in Part 7 describe each of these federal laws and summarize the types of limitations placed on employers before they may discipline or terminate an employee. Knowing these rights is important so you can protect your job and take appropriate measures if you feel that you are being treated unlawfully.

The federal laws discussed in theses pages are grouped by topics as follows: protected classes; safety, health, and medical conditions; other economic rights; conduct/privacy; and whistleblower rights.

These laws do not necessarily pertain to all employees in the U.S. Many of them apply only to companies with workforces of a certain size, excluding most "mom and pop" operations and very small employers. As an example, the Civil Rights Act of 1964, which protects employees against discrimination based on race, color, sex, national origin, and religion, only covers companies with 15 or more employees.

If you work for a small employer and a particular federal law does not cover that employer, you may be protected by a law passed in your state or local area that covers smaller employers. In Ohio, for instance, the civil rights act prohibiting discrimination covers employers with as few as four employees. The stipulations of each state vary, and some states have not passed laws that address issues covered by federal law. State laws are described generally in Part 8.

Tip: As with most legal claims, you should be aware of applicable statutes of limitations. Generally, that means that you only have a limited amount of time after you have been subjected to some form of adverse action to file either an administrative charge with a federal agency or a lawsuit. These statutes of limitations are generally enforced regardless of the reason for your delay.

RIGHTS RELATED TO PROTECTED CLASSES

Title VII of the Civil Rights Act

The most comprehensive exception to the employment-at-will doctrine is Title VII of the Civil Rights Act of 1964. It prohibits discrimination in employment based upon race, color, sex, national origin, and religion. Believe it or not, under employment at will, an employer could lawfully fire someone prior to 1964 if he or she did not like an employee's race, color, sex, national origin, or religion.

Under Title VII, an employee can bring a claim of employment discrimination for any adverse action taken by an employer, whether it is failure to hire, termination, or some form of significant discipline. Title VII governs employers with 15 or more employees, as well as all state and local governments, educational institutions, private and public employment agencies, labor organizations, and joint-labor management committees controlling apprenticeship and training.

Title VII prohibits retaliation against employees who oppose any unlawful action or practice disallowed by Title VII. For example, your employer cannot retaliate if you file a discrimination complaint with Human Resources, or if you serve as a witness for another employee who is alleging unlawful discrimination.

You may not file suit under Title VII unless you have first filed a charge of discrimination and/or retaliation with the Equal Employment Opportunity Commission within either 180 days or 300 days of your notice of the adverse action, depending upon the state in which you work.

Tip: After the EEOC has investigated your charge for at least 180 days, you may request a dismissal of the charge in order to proceed to court. If you file an age discrimination case, you may request a dismissal after 60 days.

Unlawful Harassment

Sexual harassment, racial harassment, and other harassment based on a protected characteristic are prohibited under Title VII.

As described in Part 5, sexual harassment in the workplace can be against the law under either a "quid pro quo" theory or a "hostile work environment" theory. Quid pro quo harassment occurs when submitting to or rejecting a sexual advance is used as the basis for an employment decision or is made a condition of employment. Under this theory, the harassment must result in a tangible employment action.

The second type of sexual harassment is hostile environment. An unlawful hostile environment may be actionable when conduct of a sexual nature is sufficiently severe or pervasive that it creates an intimidating, hostile, or offensive work environment. This sometimes occurs when female employees, and perhaps male employees, are subjected to verbal and/or physical conduct of a sexual nature.

Racial and other harassment based on a protected characteristic may be actionable under the hostile environment theory, and likewise requires that conduct must be sufficiently severe or pervasive that it creates an intimidating, hostile, or offensive work environment.

If you are subjected to sexual harassment or other unlawful harassment by a supervisor, the employer is strictly liable for the conduct, which means that you do not need to file an internal complaint or place the employer on notice of the harassment before filing an EEOC charge. If the racial or sexual harassment is conducted by co-workers, you are first required to place the employer on notice of your complaint and allow the employer to take "prompt, effective action."

Beware: Like other forms of discrimination under Title VII, you must first file a charge with the EEOC before filing a lawsuit for either sexual or racial harassment under federal law.

The Pregnancy Discrimination Act

In 1978, Congress amended Title VII of the Civil Rights Act of 1964 to prohibit pregnancy discrimination. Pregnancy discrimination is defined as discrimination on the basis of pregnancy, childbirth, and related conditions.

Pregnancy discrimination can occur when an employer refuses to hire a pregnant applicant, fires or demotes an employee who is pregnant, denies the same or a similar job to a pregnant employee when she returns from leave, treats a pregnant employee differently than other temporarily disabled workers, or engages in other discriminatory conduct.

Like other forms of discrimination, establishing that an employer treated a pregnant employee unfairly is not enough. Instead, pregnancy discrimination claims are generally analyzed under the disparate treatment theory of discrimination discussed in Part 3.

The Equal Pay Act and the Lilly Ledbetter Fair Pay Act

A year before Congress passed Title VII of the Civil Rights Act of 1964, it passed the Equal Pay Act of 1963. The Equal Pay Act amended the Fair Labor Standards Act (to be discussed later), and is aimed at abolishing wage disparity based on sex.

The Equal Pay Act (EPA) applies to employers with greater than $550,000 in sales per year. Complainants are not required to file an administrative charge prior to instituting a lawsuit. Under the act, you have 2 years to file a lawsuit unless the EPA violation is willful. In that event, the statute of limitations is extended to 3 years. It is often difficult to establish that an EPA violation is willful, however.

The Equal Pay Act prohibits employers from discriminating among employees on the basis of sex by paying unequal wages for equal work on jobs, the performance of which requires equal skill, effort, and responsibility, and which are performed under similar working conditions. Exceptions to the law apply when the difference in payment is based on a seniority system, a merit system, a system that measures earnings by quantity or quality of production, or is based on a factor other than sex.

If an employee can establish that different wages are paid to employees of the opposite sex, that the employees perform substantially equal work, and that the jobs are performed under similar working conditions, liability under the EPA is established regardless of the intention of the employer.

If you feel that your employer has violated the EPA, it often makes sense to file an additional charge of sex discrimination under Title VII and allege that your employer has treated you differently than employees of the opposite sex. However, regardless of the status of your EEOC charge, a claim for unequal pay under the EPA must still be brought within 2 or 3 years of the violation, as discussed above.

In 2009, Congress passed the Lilly Ledbetter Fair Pay Act, which overturned a holding of a Supreme Court case regarding the applicable statute of limitations. This law provides that each gender-unequal paycheck is a new violation of the law. Thus, if you have been the victim of an Equal Pay Act violation for many years, you may bring a claim so long as you have received at least one unequal paycheck within the last 2 or 3 years.

Section 1981 of the Civil Rights Act

Section 1981, passed in 1866, is an often overlooked statute that prohibits discrimination based on race or color, and it was essentially unenforced for a century after its passage. This legislation, which was the first major anti-discrimination employment statute, has been interpreted by the Supreme Court to protect all ethnic groups.

A four-year statute of limitations exists for Section 1981 claims, and there is no requirement to file with the EEOC or any other administrative agency before instituting a Section 1981 action in court. In addition, there is no threshold for a minimum number of employees, and both state and federal courts have jurisdiction over Section 1981.

In 1989, the Supreme Court limited the application of Section 1981 to unlawful hiring decisions, reasoning that the act was limited to the making and enforcing of contracts. Congress later passed the Civil Rights Act of 1991, which made it clear that employees could sue under Section 1981 for post-contract formation and modification conduct, including discriminatory termination.

The Age Discrimination in Employment Act

Not passed until 1967, the federal Age Discrimination in Employment Act (ADEA) prohibits employers from discriminating against employees over the age of 39. When the law was originally enacted, Congress set an upper cap of 70 years old, meaning that you could lawfully discriminate against persons over the age of 70. For example, employers could lawfully require employees to retire once they obtained the age of 70. In a subsequent amendment to the law, the upper age limit was eliminated.

In every instance, "age discrimination" is taken to mean favor granted to younger persons over older persons. In the context of the law, there is no such thing as "reverse age discrimination." Thus, while Caucasian employees and males, long viewed by many to enjoy favored employment status, are covered by federal prohibitions against sex and race discrimination, the same broad brush is not applied to younger persons who might claim they were discriminated against in favor of older employees. In a culture obsessed with youthfulness, this is one arena in which the elders emerge victorious!

Proof of age discrimination follows the same analytical framework as other forms of discrimination, either by way of a claim of disparate treatment or disparate impact, as discussed in Part 3. While claims of disparate impact are relatively infrequent, the highest percentage of disparate impact claims are based on age, such as age limits placed on public service employees due to alleged physical requirements of their jobs.

The employer size threshold for age discrimination claims under ADEA is higher than for other kinds of discrimination covered by Title VII. The ADEA is only applicable to private employers with 20 or more employees (not 15), as well as state and local governments (including school districts), employment agencies, and labor organizations.

Once you file a claim of age discrimination with the EEOC, which is a prerequisite to a lawsuit under federal law, you need only allow the EEOC 60 days to investigate a charge of age discrimination before requesting a dismissal of your charge so that you may pursue the matter in court. (Under Title VII, you must allow the EEOC at least 180 days to investigate a claim.)

The Older Workers Benefit Protection Act

One of the least appreciated employment laws in America is the Older Workers Benefit Protection Act (OWBPA). This act amended the federal law prohibiting age discrimination by safeguarding older workers' employee benefits against disparate treatment. Under this law, employers must pay the same amount for each benefit provided to an older worker as they pay for a younger worker.

The most important aspect of the law concerns the length of time allowed for employees 40 years of age or older to consider severance or early retirement offers. Employers who offer either voluntary or involuntary severance payments or early retirement benefits must allow terminated employees at least 21 calendar days (45 days in a mass layoff) to consider the offer. In addition, severance agreements must advise employees of their right to seek legal advice and to revoke their acceptance of the offer within seven days of acceptance. Employers must also provide information about the ages of both terminated and retained employees in order to help employees understand whether age may have been a factor in their termination.

The OWBPA also requires the employer to advise employees of the "decisional unit" that selected them for termination, and the employer is required to provide the criteria used for selection. Often, employers "forget" to include the criteria in a severance agreement.

This law is very important because employers were previously not required to allow employees any particular length of time in which to consider a proposed severance agreement. This gave employers an advantage, in that it limited their exposure to lawsuits. The law's 21-day period is intended to allow employees sufficient time to obtain legal advice if desired. More often than not, attorneys are able to reach an agreement with the employer to extend the deadline while the attorney gathers more information in order to evaluate the proposed release of claims.

The flip side to this law is that, once you sign a severance agreement that complies with the OWBPA and do not revoke it within 7 days, it is virtually impossible to bring an age discrimination claim later on. This holds true even if you discover facts after signing that would have supported a claim of age discrimination.

Tip: Severance agreements with 21-day deadlines require prompt legal advice. The earlier you can consult with a lawyer, the better. Make sure you tell any lawyer with whom you wish to meet of the 21-day deadline.

The Uniformed Services Employment and Reemployment Rights Act

The Uniformed Services Employment and Reemployment Rights Act (USERRA), passed in 1994, is designed to protect the civilian employment of non–full-time service members in the United States military when they are called to active duty. The law applies to all uniformed services and their respective reserve components.

USERRA applies to all employers in the United States, and to all U.S. employers operating in foreign countries. Under the law, returning service members are to be reemployed in a job that they would have attained had they not been absent for military service, with no loss of seniority, status, or pay, and they are entitled to other rights and benefits determined by seniority. This provision is known as the "escalator principle" and, if the service member cannot qualify for the escalator position, he or she is entitled to alternative reemployment.

Under USERRA, the individual who is performing military service is deemed to be on a furlough or leave of absence and is entitled to the non-seniority rights and benefits accorded other individuals on comparable types of non-military leave.

In addition, service members on duty for more than 30 days may elect to continue employer-sponsored health care for up to 24 months, so long as they pay the required premium, which is permitted to be 102% of the full premium for regular employees. If service is shorter than 31 days, health care coverage is offered as if the service member had remained employed. USERRA also protects all pension plan coverage.

When service members return from service, they must apply for reemployment or report back to work, depending upon the length of time spent on military duty. For example, if the time spent on military duty is between 30 and 181 days, the service member must submit an application for reemployment within 14 days of release from service. For longer service, the application must be submitted within 90 days.

The United States Department of Labor provides assistance to anyone with a USERRA claim. If the claim is not resolved following an investigation, the service member may have his or her claim referred to the Department of Justice for consideration of representation in an appropriate federal district court at no cost to the employee.

In 2008, Congress passed a law to make it clear that there is no statute of limitations applicable to USERRA causes of action accruing on or after October 10, 2008. The time for bringing such claims is limited only by the equitable doctrine of laches (even without a statute of limitations, this doctrine allows a defendant to claim it is unfair if you wait many years to bring a claim), and by the practical difficulty of proving one's case when one brings the case many years after the fact.

RIGHTS RELATED TO SAFETY, HEALTH, AND MEDICAL CONDITIONS

The Occupational Safety and Health Act

In 1970, Congress passed the Occupational Safety and Health Act (OSHA), and it remains the primary federal law governing workplace health and safety in the private sector, federal agencies, and the U.S. Postal Service. It excludes state and local governments, but some states have laws similar to OSHA that apply to their state and local governments. The primary goal of OSHA is to insure that employers provide employees with safe workplaces that are free from recognized hazards, exposure to toxic chemicals, excessive noise levels, mechanical dangers, heat or cold stress, and unsanitary conditions.

OSHA includes an important anti-retaliation provision applicable to employees who exercise their rights under the act. Employees are within their rights to complain to OSHA, seek an OSHA inspection, participate in an OSHA inspection, or participate in any proceeding related to an OSHA inspection. Employers are prohibited from discharging, retaliating, or discriminating against any worker for exercising rights under the act.

Unfortunately, a strict time limit of 30 days applies for filing a claim of retaliation with an OSHA Area Office representative. In states with OSHA-approved state plans, state and local government employees are also protected against retaliation, but public sector workers in these states must file their complaints for retaliation only with state plan representatives.

The Americans with Disabilities Act

In 1990, Congress passed the Americans with Disabilities Act (ADA) with the intention of eliminating employment discrimination against individuals with disabilities. The law has two components: a prohibition against discrimination and/or retaliation, and a provision requiring employers to make "reasonable accommodations" to protect the rights of employees with disabilities in all aspects of employment.

The ADA applies to employers of 15 or more employees and requires that an aggrieved individual file a charge of discrimination with the EEOC before filing a lawsuit in federal court under the ADA. State and local governments are covered regardless of size.

The anti-discrimination provisions of the ADA operate in much the same manner as the anti-discrimination and retaliation provisions of Title VII and the ADEA. The most common form of discrimination is analyzed under the disparate treatment theory discussed in Part 3.

An important component of the law is the requirement with respect to reasonable accommodations. Under this aspect of the law, covered employers are required to make accommodations for employee disabilities, such as restructuring a job, altering the layout of work stations, or modifying equipment, unless the accommodation constitutes an "undue hardship" on the employer. The undue hardship defense essentially means that larger employers have a greater responsibility to accommodate disabled employees.

In addition, the ADA prohibits employers from asking prospective employees about their medical conditions or disabilities. An employer is only allowed to ask such questions after it has made a conditional offer of employment so that an employer is aware of any necessary accommodations.

If you have a disability that requires accommodation, it is often advisable to make such a request in writing to your employer. If you do so, you should make clear that you are open to any reasonable accommodations; an employer is required to engage in an interactive process with you to discuss ways to reasonably accommodate a particular disability.

You are covered by the ADA if you have a physical or mental impairment that substantially limits one or more of your major life activities, or you have a record of such an impairment, or your employer regards you as having such an impairment even if you do not have an impairment. Often, the key question involves an analysis of how your medical condition limits one or more of your major life activities.

Other persons protected by the law are those who have an association with an individual know to have a disability, such as a parent, or those who are subjected to retaliation for assisting people with disabilities and asserting their rights under the ADA.

The Family and Medical Leave Act

One of the most controversial federal laws passed by Congress to protect employees with medical conditions or certain family needs is the Family and Medical Leave Act (FMLA). This act, which passed in 1993, requires employers covered by the law to provide employees job-protected unpaid leave for qualified medical and family reasons.

You are eligible for FMLA benefits only if your employer has 50 or more employees within a 75-mile radius of your work site. All private-sector employers with 50 or more employees must comply with FMLA regulations. The law also applies to all public agencies, including state, local, and federal employers and local education agencies (schools) no matter their size. You are not covered by the FMLA until you have worked for a company subject to the act for at least 12 months and 1,250 hours during the last 12 months. Thus, many short-term and part-time employees are not covered by the FMLA.

The FMLA only provides unpaid leaves of absence, although you are allowed to use accrued paid leave at the same time as your unpaid leave to the extent that you have such time available to you.

The FMLA allows unpaid leave for up to 12 weeks a year for your own serious illness, to care for a seriously ill family member, to care for a new child (whether for the birth of a child or for placement of a child through adoption or foster care), to care for an injured service member in the family, or to address qualifying exigencies arising out of a family member's deployment into the armed services.

When you return from an approved leave under the FMLA, your employer is required to return you to the same position unless that position is no longer available. In that event, you must be provided with a position that is substantially equal in pay, benefits, and responsibility. In addition, your employee benefits are protected while you are on leave, and you are entitled to reinstatement of all benefits upon your return.

One of the most important aspects of the FMLA is the protection against retaliation for exercising rights under the act. Exercising your rights includes making a request for FMLA leave or taking an FMLA leave.

Many states have enacted their own FMLAs that have a lower threshold for employer coverage. For example, Oregon and the District of Columbia have reduced the threshold to 25 and 20 employees, respectively. Some states have expanded the definition of family to allow for greater latitude in taking a leave. California, for instance, defines family to include a domestic partner and a domestic partner's child, and Hawaii includes a grandparent, parent-in-law, grandparent-in-law, and an employee's "reciprocal beneficiary" (domestic partner).

Some states have even passed FMLA-type statutes to give parents unpaid leave to attend their child's educational activities. These include California, the District of Columbia, Massachusetts, Minnesota, Rhode Island, and Vermont. Other states, including Massachusetts and Vermont, have passed statutes to give workers unpaid leave to take family members to routine medical visits. Still others have passed FMLA-type statutes to give workers unpaid leave to address the affects of domestic violence, stalking, or sexual assault, including Colorado, Florida, Hawaii, and Illinois.

Employees who have a grievance about any aspect of their FMLA leave (including the failure to have been granted one) may file a federal claim. There is a two-year statute of limitations for federal FMLA claims, although the statute can be extended to three years if the violation is willful.

The Rehabilitation Act

Seventeen years before Congress granted broad protection to individuals with disabilities through the passage of the Americans with Disabilities Act, a more limited law was passed in Section 504 of the Rehabilitation Act of 1973. This act applies only to the federal government, employers with federal contracts or subcontracts, programs conducted by federal agencies, and institutions receiving federal funds, such as colleges and universities.

The standards for determining employment discrimination under the Rehabilitation Act are the same as those used in the Americans with Disabilities Act. In addition, the act requires affirmative action on behalf of persons with disabilities.

The Rehabilitation Act does not contain a statute of limitations. Thus, courts applying the act will look to the most analogous state law and apply that statute of limitations. Many courts have applied a particular state's statute of limitations for personal injury claims to claims under the Rehabilitation Act.

RIGHTS RELATED TO OTHER ECONOMIC ISSUES

The Fair Labor Standards Act

One of the most significant economic pieces of employment legislation passed by Congress is the Fair Labor Standards Act (FLSA). Under this act, covered employers are required to pay minimum wage and overtime pay, and must keep employee time and pay records. As of July 2009, the minimum wage is $7.25 per hour. Overtime pay is calculated at a rate of one and one-half times the regular rate of pay for hours worked over 40 hours in a workweek.

Many states also have minimum wage and overtime laws and, if an employee is subject to both federal and state minimum wage laws, the employee is entitled to the higher minimum wage.

While hourly paid workers are entitled to overtime pay, one of the myths of the American workplace is that "salaried" workers are not entitled to overtime. Exploiting this myth, some companies promote workers from "hourly" to "salaried" positions with the understanding that, in exchange for the salary, the worker gives up her right to overtime pay. Because these "salaried" job titles often carry an elevated status within the workplace, working without overtime may seem reasonable to the worker.

The FLSA exempts certain executive, administrative, professional, outside sales and computer employees from the entitlement to time-and-one-half overtime benefits. These exemptions are commonly referred to as the "white collar" exemptions, and they have spawned substantial litigation as some American companies choose to push the envelope in increasingly aggressive efforts to deny overtime pay to workers and their families.

The white-collar exemptions—like all FLSA exemptions—are narrowly construed against the employer. To utilize a white-collar exemption, a company generally must clear two independent hurdles. First, the employee must be paid on a "salaried basis" at a salary of at least $455 per week. Second, if the worker is paid a salary, an analysis of the worker's job duties must reveal that she actually works as an executive, administrative, professional, outside sales, or computer employee, as those terms are defined under the FLSA.

To qualify for the "executive employee" exemption, the following criteria must be established: (i) the worker's primary duty must be managing the enterprise or managing a customarily recognized department or subdivision of the enterprise; (ii) the worker must customarily and regularly direct the work of at least two or more other full-time employees or their equivalent; and (iii) the worker must have the authority to hire or fire other employees, or the employee's suggestions and recommendations as to the hiring, firing, advancement, promotion or any other change of status of other employees must be given particular weight.

To qualify for the "administrative employee" exemption, the employee's primary duty (i) must be the performance of office or non-manual work directly related to the management or general business operations of the employer or the employer's customers; and (ii) must include the exercise of discretion and independent judgment with respect to matters of significance.

Workers are classified as exempt "professional employees" if their "primary duty is the performance of work (i) requiring knowledge of an advanced type in a field of science or learning customarily acquired by a prolonged course of specialized intellectual instruction; or (ii) requiring invention, imagination, originality or talent in a recognized field of artistic or creative endeavor." The regulations also exempt "[c]omputer systems analysts, computer programmers, software engineers or other similarly skilled workers in the computer field," as well as most "outside salesmen," and most employees with a total annual compensation in excess of $100,000.

In addition to the white-collar exemptions, the FLSA contains various statutory exemptions for other types of workers. These exemptions include:

- Workers (such as truck drivers) employed by common carriers and whose qualifications and maximum hours are dictated by the federal Motor Carrier Act;
- Most newspaper delivery drivers;

- Many chartered bus drivers;
- Taxicab drivers;
- Most railroad and airline employees;
- Workers employed in certain "amusement or recreational establishment[s], organized camp[s], or religious or non-profit educational conference center[s]";
- "Seamen" and certain workers employed in the fishing and seafood industry;
- Most agricultural workers;
- Most workers employed by small-market news publications; and
- Babysitters and certain domestic service workers "employed on a casual basis."

Under federal overtime law, a workweek is any fixed and regularly recurring period of 168 hours—7 consecutive 24-hour periods—and there is no limit on the number of hours employees 16 years and older may be required to work. Unless you exceed 40 hours in the relevant workweek, the FLSA does not require overtime pay for work on weekends, holidays, or regular days of rest.

In general, "hours worked" includes all the time during which an employee is required to be on an employer's premises, on duty, or at a prescribed workplace. The FLSA applies to all employers engaged in in-state commerce or in the production of goods for commerce, including private-sector businesses and public agencies.

There is a two-year statute of limitations under the Fair Labor Standards Act, which can extend to three years if the violation is willful. There is no requirement to file an administrative charge with any government agency before initiating a lawsuit.

Section 510 of the Employee Retirement Income Security Act

Section 510 of the 1974 Employee Retirement Income Security Act (ERISA) makes it unlawful to discharge, fine, suspend, discipline, or discriminate against a participant in an employee benefit plan for exercising any right to which he or she is entitled. Under ERISA, it is also illegal to interfere with the attainment of any right to which a plan participant may become entitled.

An ERISA plan is either an employee welfare benefit plan or an employee pension benefit plan. Employee welfare benefit plans are employee benefit plans established or maintained by your company that provide welfare benefits, such as medical, disability, and death benefits. Pension benefit plans, or retirement plans, are employee benefit plans established or maintained by your company that provide retirement income to you or result in a deferral of income by you for periods extending to the termination of employment or beyond.

For a claim to be successful under ERISA Section 510, you must show that the alleged discrimination was intended either to retaliate for exercise of a right or to interfere with the attainment of an entitled right.

ERISA permits legal claims by plan participants or beneficiaries or fiduciaries. There is no specific statute of limitations under ERISA, and courts look to the most analogous state law's statute of limitations to determine the appropriate statue of limitations in any particular ERISA claim. You are not required to file a claim with any government agency prior to bringing a lawsuit under ERISA, but you do not have a right to a jury trial.

The Worker Adjustment and Retraining Notification Act

The Worker Adjustment and Retraining Notification Act (WARN) is a 1988 law that protects employees by requiring most employers with 100 or more employees to provide 60 calendar days' advance notification of plant closings and mass layoffs. Such a notice must be provided to managers and supervisors, hourly employees, and salaried workers.

Employees who have worked fewer than 6 months in the last 12-month work period or have worked fewer than 20 hours per week on average are excluded from the 100-employee minimum.

The WARN Act does not apply if a plant closing or a mass layoff results in fewer than 50 employees losing their jobs at a single employment site, a layoff is for six months or less, or work hours are not reduced at least 50 percent in each month of any six-month period. The act also does not apply if 50 to 499 workers lose their jobs and the number of terminations is less than one-third of the employer's total, active workforce at a single employment site.

There are three exceptions to the 60-day notice requirement, although the notice still must be provided as soon as practical even when these exceptions apply. The three exceptions are so-called faltering companies that are actively seeking capital or business and believe that advance notice would preclude their ability to obtain such capital or business, other unforeseeable business circumstances beyond an employer's control, or a natural disaster.

A company that violates the WARN Act is liable to each employee for an amount equal to back pay and benefits for the period of the violation up to 60 days. There is no requirement that employees file an administrative charge with a government agency, and both individual and class action suits are permissible. A court may allow reasonable attorneys' fees as part of any final judgment. Several states and localities have passed their own WARN acts as well.

RIGHTS RELATED TO CONDUCT/PRIVACY

The National Labor Relations Act

The first major piece of federal legislation creating an exception to the employment-at-will doctrine was the National Labor Relations Act (NLRA), which was passed during the Great Depression in 1935. The law applies to all private employers engaged in interstate commerce with 15 or more employees. Excluded from coverage are employees covered by the Railway Labor Act, agricultural and domestic employees, supervisors, and some close relatives of individual employers.

The primary aim of this legislation was to encourage the practice of collective bargaining and protect the exercise by employees of full freedom of association, self-organization, and designation of representatives of their own choosing, all for the purpose of negotiating the terms and conditions of their employment or other mutual aid or protection. The law protects a wide range of activities, whether a union is involved or not, in order to promote organization and collective bargaining.

In addition to protecting workers in connection with the process by which a union is organized, or in connection with the continued operation of a union, the law also protects non-union employees who engage in pro-tected, concerted activities while working for an employer. Thus, even non-union employees are protected by the NLRA if they are acting on behalf of more than one employee.

This law is enforced by the National Labor Relations Board (NLRB), and a charge must be filed and served within six months of the alleged violation.

The Employee Polygraph Protection Act

As a result of the general unreliability of polygraph examinations, the Employee Polygraph Protection Act (EPPA) was passed in 1988 to prohibit most private employers from using lie detector tests, either for pre-employment screening or during the course of employment. In addition, an employer may not discriminate or retaliate against an employee or job applicant who refuses to take a test or exercises other rights under the law.

There are limited exceptions to the EPPA. For example, the act permits polygraph tests to be administered to job applicants of pharmaceutical manufacturers, distributors, and dispensers, as well as certain job applicants of security service firms. In other circumstances, the act allows lie detector tests with certain employees who are reasonably suspected of involvement in workplace theft or embezzlement that results in specific economic loss or injury to the employer. Permissible polygraph examinations are subject to strict standards for the conduct of the test, including the pretest, testing and post-testing phases.

The law does not apply to governmental employers, businesses under contract with the federal government for counterintelligence work, or employers who have a significant impact on the health or safety of any state (for example, power plants, water works, and toxic waste disposal sites).

The EPPA has a statute of limitations of three years.

The Consumer Credit Protection Act

The Consumer Credit Protection Act of 1968 protects you from discharge by your employer because your wages have been garnished for any one debt. The law also limits the amount of your earnings that may be garnished in any one week.

This law protects everyone receiving personal earnings, whether in the form of wages, salaries, commissions, bonuses, or other income. The garnishment restrictions do not apply to certain bankruptcy court orders, or to debts due for federal or state taxes.

The United States Department of Labor enforces the act, but the applicable statute of limitations varies from state to state.

The Juror Protection Act

The 1978 Juror Protection Act (JPA) protects you if you are called for jury service in any federal court. Some states have also passed laws to protect you if you are called for jury service in a state court.

The Juror Protection Act applies to all employers, and a federal district court has the power to appoint counsel to represent you in any district court action necessary to resolve a claim under the JPA.

There is no specific statute of limitations contained within the Juror Protection Act, but you should not delay if you believe your employer has either discriminated or retaliated against you because of your jury service or your scheduled jury service.

Genetic Information Nondiscrimination Act

The Genetic Information Nondiscrimination Act (GINA) was passed in 2008 to prohibit employers and health insurers from discriminating based on employees' or potential employees' genetic composition. Entities subject to the law include all private employers, state and local governments, education institutions that employ 15 or more employees, private and public employment agencies, labor organizations, and joint labor management committees controlling apprenticeship and training.

There is a time limit of 180 or 300 days to initiate a claim, depending on your state.

WHISTLEBLOWER RIGHTS

Introduction to Whistleblowing Laws

There is extensive legislation on the federal, state, and local levels that protects employees who "blow the whistle" on their employers. Some of the more commonly invoked federal statutes are described in the following sections, but you should be aware that there are a significant number of other laws and court decisions that prohibit retaliation against employees who appropriately disclose employer misconduct.

Many local and state laws provide broader protection than the federal statutes. Because of the number of potential laws that may be applicable, you should consult with a lawyer in your locality to determine whether any law protects you in your particular situation.

Whistleblowing can be dangerous because of the very real threat of retaliation and the natural tendency of the accused to dispute your truthfulness or motives for raising the issue. Thus, it is wise that you consult with counsel before making a complaint as a "whistleblower" to ensure that you have legal protection against retaliation.

Many employees wrongly believe that any employer misconduct, breach of ethics, or violation of law is protected. In general, protected complaints focus on employer activities that cause damage to public safety, waste tax dollars, violate the public's trust in government, or involve corporate financial fraud. Moreover, some laws require that whistleblowers follow specific steps in order to gain protection against adverse treatment as a result of a complaint, such as various "fair play" provisions that require a whistleblower to give his or her employer an opportunity to fix the problem.

Most whistleblowers must establish that they engaged in protected activity, which means that they reported a violation or took some other action to help enforce the law. In addition, you, as a whistleblower, must show that the employer knew or believed you took the protected activity and that thereafter you suffered an adverse employment action because of your protected activity.

Each of the whistleblower laws sets a time limit to bring your complaint and, in some cases, the time limits are very short. For example, whistleblower claims under federal environmental laws require that a written complaint be filed with the Occupational Safety and Health Administration within 30 days of an adverse action.

Tip: The National Whistleblowers Center maintains a Lawyer Referral Service in Washington, D.C., and information may be obtained by e-mailing info@whistleblowers.org. In addition, the Government Accountability Project is a national organization that provides advocacy and legal support to whistleblowers. It is located in Seattle, Washington.

The Whistleblower Protection Act

Federal employees who engage in whistleblowing are protected by the Whistleblower Protection Act of 1989 (WPA) if an illegal form of retaliation occurs, e.g., a government agency takes an adverse action against you for your whistleblowing activity involving a federal government entity.

Federal employees may blow the whistle by reporting a violation to a supervisor, the Inspector General, or the Office of Special Counsel. Reporting a possible violation to a supervisor or other agency official is the least formal method of whistleblowing. In addition, if your normal duties and responsibilities involve the reporting of violations, you may not be protected when reporting improprieties to your supervisor.

Contacting the Inspector General's office at the agency where the violation occurred will not necessarily result in an investigation of your allegations, and your confidentiality may not be protected because of the relationship between the Inspector General's office and agency management. Nonetheless, if you suffer retaliation because you made the disclosure, you retain your right to pursue a personal whistleblower remedy.

The Office of Special Counsel is an independent federal agency that investigates and prosecutes cases of illegal personnel practices brought to its attention by government employees. This office operates a confidential Whistleblower Disclosure Hotline (800-572-2249) and accepts reports by mail or e-mail. The advantage to contacting this office is that confidentiality is provided by law, and your complaint may result in a report being sent to the president, Congress, and/or the Comptroller General.

The False Claims Act

The earliest law to control fraud in federal contracts was enacted in 1863 and is called the False Claims Act. This act has been amended since then and in 1986 was strengthened to increase the incentives for private citizens to uncover and fight fraud. Some states have passed similar laws concerning fraud and state government contracts.

Some of the actions that violate the False Claims Act include intentionally presenting a false or fraudulent claim for payment to the federal government, charging the government for costs not related to a grant awarded by the government, or billing Medicare and Medicaid for services that were not provided or that were unnecessary.

Waste and mismanagement by government contractors, as well as tax fraud, is not prohibited conduct under the False Claims Act. Those types of violations may be covered by other federal laws.

The act allows any person who discovers that a government contractor is defrauding the federal government to report the fraud, and then sue the organization committing the fraud on behalf of the United States. The act's protections extend to employees and non-employees of the organization in question. However, there are specialized procedures to follow before bringing an action. In False Claims Act lawsuits, which are known as *qui tam* actions, a private citizen begins the litigation and the government has the right to intervene in the lawsuit. The whistleblower shares in the proceeds if the government is able to collect from the fraudulent contractor. If the government declines to intervene, the whistleblower may proceed on his or her own.

The False Claims Act also includes a prohibition against retaliation, to protect a whistleblower who makes False Claims Act–protected disclosures or files a *qui tam* suit.

Tip: The False Claims Act has many complicated components that can harm those who pursue such a claim without counsel. Some courts have even ruled that whistleblowers cannot prosecute qui tam *actions on their own without a lawyer because that would be acting as an attorney for the government. Thus, it is advisable to retain an attorney experienced in False Claims Act matters in order to be successful.*

The Sarbanes-Oxley and Dodd-Frank Acts

The Sarbanes-Oxley Act (SOX) was passed by Congress in 2002 in response to corporate fraud scandals, and it requires publicly traded companies to make new certifications about their finances. Corporate officials and employees may be personally liable if certifications are false, and such fraud could subject them to imprisonment.

The Dodd-Frank Wall Street Reform and Consumer Protection Act (Dodd-Frank Act) was enacted in 2010 and provides several protections for corporate whistleblowers. The Securities and Exchange Commission is empowered to pay an award to whistleblowers who provide original information about violations of federal securities law.

These laws protect you if you contact law enforcement authorities, if you refuse to follow illegal orders, if you object to supervisors about violations, or if you associate with others who have blown the whistle. The laws also provide protection against retribution from wrongdoers, and permit lawsuits for wrongful termination, suspension, harassment, or other discrimination that may occur because of the whistleblowers' conduct.

Employees of publicly traded companies, as well as their subsidiaries and affiliates, are protected by these laws. Dodd-Frank also protects employees in the financial services industry who report fraud or unlawful conduct related to consumer financial products or services.

You must file a complaint under these laws with the Occupational Safety and Health Administration within 180 calendar days from the date that you first learned about management's final decision to impose an adverse action. These types of time limitations are strictly enforced.

Environmental Whistleblower Laws

There are seven major federal environmental laws that protect whistleblowers who expose public health and safety violations. These seven laws are the Water Pollution Control Act, the Safe Drinking Water Act, the Toxic Substances Control Act, the Solid Waste Disposal Act, the Clean Air Act, the Energy Reorganization Act of 1974, and the Comprehensive Environmental Response, Compensation and Liability Act of 1980.

Congress passed these laws because the best source for information about what a company is actually doing is often its own employees, and people who help enforce the laws should not suffer retaliation as a result.

These laws are enforced by the Occupational Safety and Health Administration, and OSHA prefers to receive complaints at a local office. There is a short time limit of only 30 calendar days to file a whistleblower complaint with OSHA. This time period begins on the date that you first learned about management's final decision to impose the adverse action.

Food Safety Modernization Act

The Food Safety Modernization Act (FSMA) was passed in 2010 and includes protection for employees who report food safety concerns, with the goal of helping to avoid food contamination leading to illness or death. The FSMA applies to all workers engaged in the manufacture, processing, packing, transporting, distribution, reception, holding, or importation of food. It encourages employees to report safety issues without fear of being punished by their employer for blowing the whistle.

These complaints must be filed with the Occupational Safety and Health Administration within 180 days after the date on which the adverse action took place.

Part 8

State and Local Exceptions to
Employment at Will

Overview of State Law Rights

In addition to rights created by the federal government, each state has its own set of laws enacted by its respective state legislatures ("statutory law"), as well as "common law" (also known as "judge-made law"). Understandably, these laws vary widely from state to state. The following pages describe the most common state law protections, either by way of statute or common law.

Most states, but not all, have passed anti-discrimination statutes that bar discrimination on the basis of race, color, sex, national origin, religion, pregnancy, and age. Some state laws apply to employers smaller than those covered by federal law. Some have also gone further than the federal government and enacted protections based on characteristics such as sexual preference and marital status.

Many states, but not all, also provide anti-retaliation protection to employees who suffer work-related injuries covered by the state's workers' compensation law, or engage in whistleblowing of illegal, criminal, or unsafe working conditions. Others (for example, Indiana) offer protection against "blacklisting" former employees to keep them from gaining other employment.

If you work for a large employer, knowing your federal rights should be of paramount concern. However, you should also be aware that your state may provide additional protection against unfair treatment on the job.

Sexual Orientation Laws

Sexual orientation discrimination is not covered by federal laws that prohibit employment discrimination, although there are efforts to pass a federal law to make discrimination on the basis of sexual orientation illegal. These efforts include the introduction of the Employment Non-Discrimination Act (ENDA).

Sexual orientation discrimination means discrimination on the basis of an individual being lesbian, gay, bisexual, or straight. Discrimination on the basis of sexual orientation may also include someone who is discriminated against on the basis of sex, gender identity, disability (such as actual or perceived HIV status) and/or marital status.

Twenty states and hundreds of counties and cities have laws prohibiting sexual orientation discrimination. For information as to whether you are protected by these laws, you should check with an employment attorney or a local gay legal or political organization.

While current federal law does not cover sexual orientation discrimination, many federal government employees are covered by provisions in the Civil Service Reform Act of 1978. This act makes it illegal for any employer to discriminate against employees or job applicants on the basis of conduct that does not adversely affect employee performance, and this language has been interpreted to prohibit decisions based upon sexual orientation.

Because laws vary from state to state, you should investigate promptly whether you are protected if you suspect that you are the victim of sexual orientation discrimination. There are various statutes of limitations that may be applicable in your jurisdiction.

Transgender Discrimination

Discrimination based on gender identity is not specifically prohibited by federal employment discrimination laws, although the Equal Employment Opportunity Commission issued an opinion on April 25, 2012, saying that "intentional discrimination against a transgender individual because that person is transgender is, by definition, discrimination 'based on ... sex' and such discrimination therefore violates Title VII." Since some federal courts have applied a similar analysis, it is possible that a court in your jurisdiction will also conclude that transgender individuals are protected by laws prohibiting sex discrimination. While courts are not obligated to follow the EEOC's opinion, various courts defer to the EEOC about issues of employment discrimination.

The term "transgender" is used to describe someone who does not conform to stereotypes of gender identity and/or gender expression. It includes cross dressers, transvestites, drag queens and kings, female and male impersonators, intersexed individuals, pre-operative, post-operative, and non-operative transsexuals, masculine females, feminine males, and all other persons whose perceived gender or anatomic sex may be incongruent with their gender expression. It also includes persons who are perceived to be androgynous.

Eight states have anti-discrimination laws that specifically make it illegal to discriminate on the basis of transgendered status, and a growing number of cities and counties have passed similar laws. There are numerous legislative efforts around the country to add gender identity to state and local laws, government regulations, and corporate policies. Because of the ever-changing landscape, you should not delay in contacting an attorney if you suspect that you are being discriminated against based on your transgender status.

Breach of Contract: Oral and Written Contracts

A contract is an agreement between two or more parties to do something, with each party agreeing to refrain from taking action or agreeing to take some action. Lawyers call each party's provision of something valuable in exchange for the other's promise as "consideration."

In the employment setting, you have at least one contract with your employer. You agree to perform certain services and your employer agrees to pay you for your services. In many instances, that is the only contract with your employer.

Some employees—usually higher-ranking officials—have formal employment contracts outlining the expectations of both parties, the employees' pay and benefits, and post-employment obligations. However, employer handbooks, policy manuals, job offer letters, and other documents may create employment contracts that are either "express" contracts or implied contracts.

Contract claims based on handbooks and policy are often difficult to maintain, particularly if your employer includes written disclaimers of its intention to be contractually bound by the writings. Nonetheless, you should carefully review those documents.

Oral contracts are just as valid as written contracts; they are just harder to prove because of disputes of who said what, and when.

If your employer breaks a contract with you, you may sue for a "breach," or violation. Generally, contract claims do not allow for recovery beyond the terms of the contract; each party bears its own legal fees and expenses, regardless of who wins, and other compensatory, emotional distress, and punitive damages are not available.

The statute of limitations for these claims is governed by state law, and alleged breaches of oral contracts generally have shorter limitation periods.

Tip: If your boss or company makes a promise to you, you should document the circumstances completely. In some situations, you may want to send a confirmation note or e-mail ("Joe, thanks for the discussion today. I understand that we have an agreement that I will receive the promotion to Senior Clerk if I meet my goals this quarter. I understand that the following goals have been established: {list the goals as specifically as possible.}").

Promissory Estoppel

An alternative to a breach of contract theory arises when one party makes a specific statement or promise to do something, and the other party reasonably relies on the promise to her detriment. This is called an "equitable" claim and is enforceable if it would be unfair not to enforce the promise.

In the employment context, this type of claim can arise as a result of any number of statements by a boss, but the classic example is in the context of an employment offer. An employer recruits someone for a job, offers the position knowing the candidate will resign his current position, and then rescinds or significantly changes the offer. If that happens and the employee cannot regain his position with his now former employer, a claim for promissory estoppel may exist.

Like contract claims, damages are generally limited to the value of the promise, which usually means lost wages, and would not include emotional distress, punitive damages, or an attorneys' fee award.

The statutes of limitations for these claims are governed by state law and may vary widely.

Tip: If you lose a job or job opportunity as a result of a breach of contract or have a claim for promissory estoppel, you have a duty to mitigate (lessen) your losses by looking for another job opportunity. This duty applies in any type of employment termination claim as well.

Breach of Public Policy

Some states have recognized another exception to employment at will based on public policy. This type of claim arises when an employer's conduct is such that it violates a state law, a state constitution, or otherwise breaches some important policy expressed or implied by the state. These types of claims have been more broadly recognized in the last two decades.

Common examples of a violation of public policy, if recognized in your state, are such things as being fired for testifying truthfully in a court proceeding, reporting violations of safety laws, or reporting a crime to law enforcement officials.

The statute of limitations to bring such a claim is governed by state law, and remedies beyond lost wages are generally available.

Tip: It is wise to consult with a lawyer before engaging in conduct that you think may be protected by public policy because each "public policy" has its own requirements for you to meet in order to be protected.

Intentional Infliction of Emotional Distress

These claims are rarely viable, but arise if an employer's conduct is "extreme and outrageous" with the intent (or what could have been reasonably foreseen) to cause serious emotional distress, and, in fact, does cause you serious mental distress.

This type of claim is often coupled with federal or state law claims of racial or sexual harassment, and the remedies often overlap with each other.

The statute of limitations is governed by your state's laws.

Defamation

It has often been said that if employees could sue their employers for making false statements, we would need a courthouse on every street corner. Claims of false statements commonly arise in the context of discipline and performance reviews.

In fact, claims of defamation are rarely successful. First, you must prove that the maker of the statement knew it was false, or was reckless in making the statement, and was acting with malice or a spirit of ill will, hatred, or revenge. Most importantly, the statement must be "published" by making it to a third person, e.g., a prospective employer. Generally, statements within the four walls of a corporation are not "published."

Opinions cannot form the basis for defamation claims. "I think Mary wasn't very committed to her job" is an example of a statement of opinion.

Finally, even if you show the difficult elements of the claim summarized above, you must also prove that your reputation was damaged. Some statements are obviously injurious ("Bill was a serial sexual harasser"), but others require proof that persons believed the statement and thought less of you as a result. Many false statements are simply not believed by co-workers, friends, family, and others in the community.

The statute of limitations for defamation varies from state to state, but is generally at least one year.

False Imprisonment

Claims of false imprisonment are unlikely to arise, but exist when your freedom of movement is restricted ("stay in this office until I allow you to leave") without your permission or without legal justification. Often, the length of the detention is critical, as well as the reason.

These claims occasionally arise in the context of workplace investigations, when employees are interrogated about workplace issues. Generally, an employer is permitted to require you to answer work-related questions during an investigation, but extreme cases sometime occur.

The statute of limitations is governed by state law, and is generally the same as your state's limitations period for personal injury cases.

Fraud

If you suffer damages as a result of your employer telling you something that he or she knew was false, with the intent of hurting you, you could have a claim for fraud. These claims are uncommon, but sometimes arise in the context of job recruitment efforts, as in, "If you move to Omaha, we'll have a job that pays you $50,000 per year." If it turns out that the job will only pay you $30,000, you might have a claim for fraud.

These claims are rare, and are governed by your state's statute of limitations.

Assault and Battery

An assault occurs when another person attempts to touch you without your consent. A successful attempt to contact you in a way that is harmful to you or is insulting or offensive is a battery. These claims are most often coupled with claims of sexual harassment, but may exist if a supervisor or security guard makes physical contact with you without your permission.

Of course, whether you are actually injured is critical. Many assaults and batteries occur without any resulting damage; in these cases, it is impractical to pursue the claim unless it is coupled with some other claim.

Most workplace injuries are covered by your state's workers' compensation system, but some states allow claims outside of workers' compensation for intentional injuries. Claims for assault or battery are governed by state law.

Interference with a Business Relationship

Some persons, particularly in the context of restrictive covenants, find themselves in a situation involving a former employer affecting their current employment. If you have a job, and a third party interferes with that job without justification, you may have a claim for interference with your business relationship.

For example, if you signed a non-compete and a non-solicitation covenant with your former employer, and your former employer wrongly attempts to stop you from working in the future, you may have a claim. Often, this occurs when a former employer or its lawyer sends a threatening letter to your current employer, wrongly stating that your employment is in violation of one or more restrictions.

Another example of this type of claim could occur if a third party, such as an ex-friend, falsely reports something to your employer that results in discharge.

This claim is governed by your state's statute of limitations.

Negligence

Legal claims based on another's failure to exercise reasonable care are usually thought of in the context of personal injury claims resulting from automobile accidents. In rare cases, not including injuries at work that are covered by workers' compensation laws, you may bring a negligence claim against your employer.

Examples of possible claims based on a negligence theory are negligent infliction of severe emotional distress (sometimes coupled with claims of unlawful harassment), negligent retention of a company supervisor or employee (such as an employer maintaining the employment of a supervisor known to the employer to be a sexual harasser), or negligent hiring (again, commonly used in the context of hiring someone the employer knows is a sexual harasser).

If these types of claims are available, your employer may have insurance to cover its liability, and the availability of insurance is often a factor in settlement of claims. For most employment claims, such as claims of discrimination, employers only have insurance coverage if they have purchased what is called Employment Practices Liability Insurance. Most companies elect not to have such coverage.

Part 9

Obtaining Legal Advice

Do I Need A Lawyer?

If you have been treated unlawfully on the job, you almost always need a lawyer. Abraham Lincoln, the 16th president of the United States, is often quoted as saying, "He who represents himself has a fool for a lawyer."

The primary benefit of retaining an employment lawyer is that a lawyer will be able to provide counsel and advice not only on the law, but also on the practical aspects of challenging a particular action by an employer. Moreover, a lawyer is in a position to provide you with a more objective viewpoint about your situation and the options available to you.

A lawyer also provides some leverage if you desire to reach a compromise. Retaining a lawyer sends a message as to your commitment to challenge a particular action, because employers know that retaining a lawyer is not easy and involves an investment of time and money. If you do not have a lawyer representing you in an employment matter, you may not be taken as seriously, perhaps because your employer thinks that you tried unsuccessfully to find a lawyer who was willing to represent you.

How Do I Find the Right Lawyer?

In most situations involving employment law, you should seek a lawyer with experience in employment law rather than a general practitioner or a lawyer who works in another area of law.

The best source for finding a lawyer is likely another lawyer. Attorneys working in your community will probably know lawyers who practice employment law. So start by contacting a lawyer you know personally.

A second source for finding the right lawyer is through a local bar association. Bar associations across the country have lawyer referral services to assist the public with finding attorneys in particular areas of practice. Often, they refer a lawyer who has agreed to charge a reduced consultation fee.

A third source is the National Employment Lawyers Association (NELA) and its website, NELA.org. NELA is a national organization comprised of many of the most experienced employment lawyers in the country, and it may be able to provide a referral in your community.

The last source for finding a local lawyer is through the Internet or your local Yellow Pages.

Tip: When you are looking for an employment lawyer, consult with more than one potential lawyer or law firm. Many lawyers make it a practice of giving referrals to at least three lawyers. The reason is simple: while it is time consuming to meet more than one lawyer, interviewing or meeting more than one gives you an opportunity to find the one with whom you are most comfortable and who is most experienced in handling cases like yours.

What Can I Expect a Lawyer to Do for Me?

An employment lawyer will review the facts of your situation and determine whether it is worthwhile for her—and you—to pursue the matter further. Rarely can a lawyer tell you whether you will have a successful case from a first meeting; rather, she can tell you whether your situation deserves to be investigated.

If you retain a lawyer to represent you, you should expect her to review the matter as thoroughly as possible, including evaluating whatever your employer will provide, and making a recommendation as to a course of action. Possible options include negotiating with your current or former employer to settle your claim, assisting you with the filing of any required administrative charge or claim, comparing a proposed settlement offer with the lawyer's evaluation of the value of your potential claim, and offering to represent you in litigation.

Once a lawyer evaluates your situation thoroughly, she should advise you of the costs (including legal fees and expenses), risks, and benefits of proceeding with a lawsuit. During the representation, you should expect your lawyer to advise you periodically of any progress and the status of her representation. The wheels of justice grind slowly, so patience is a virtue. Do not expect your lawyer to be available whenever you want—or you likely have a lawyer with not much to do!

Given the importance of choosing the right employment lawyer for your situation, several tips apply.

Tip 1: The old adage, "If you want something done, find a busy person" applies equally well when you want something done in the legal system.

Tip 2: A basic, reasonable expectation of your lawyer is that she should make a recommendation to you whenever an important decision, such as whether to accept a settlement offer, needs to be made. You should take your attorney's recommendation seriously, and while you should usually defer to your lawyer's advice on strategy, a decision on settlement is your decision, not your attorney's. Good faith differences occur during representation.

Tip 3: If you are unhappy with your lawyer, seek a second opinion before it is too late. Your relationship with your lawyer must be based on trust, and it is important that the lawyer you choose has your full confidence.

How Much Will I Be Charged by a Lawyer?

Most employment lawyers will charge a flat fee for an initial consultation to meet you and review preliminary information. Charges for the initial consultation vary widely, and you should make sure you have a clear understanding of each lawyer's consultation fee before making an appointment.

If an employment lawyer offers to represent you, he will discuss whether he will charge on a contingency fee–basis (meaning the fee is determined by applying a percentage—usually 33–40%—of the amount recovered), an hourly fee–basis, or some other basis. Some employment lawyers will offer a "flat fee" to cover the representation, which should be based on the expected range of hourly fees you will incur.

Any fee arrangement should be in writing and should clearly state how the fees will be calculated and when they will be due. In addition, it should state who is responsible for any out-of-pocket expenses, and should specify the scope of the representation. Does it just include the investigation of your claims, or does it also cover litigation, if warranted?

Be wary if an employment lawyer only offers to represent you on an hourly fee–basis. If the lawyer is confident of a successful resolution, why wouldn't he want to share the risk of an unsuccessful outcome? Of course, sometimes it is in your best interest to hire a lawyer on an hourly fee–basis, particularly if you expect a good result in a short period of time.

Tip: If you hire a lawyer on an hourly fee–basis, ask the lawyer for a written estimate of fees. While it is often difficult to know precisely how much time will be involved, an experienced employment lawyer should give you a fair approximation. You should monitor monthly statements with the estimate in mind.

So, You've Decided to Hire a Lawyer: What's Next?

If you believe you have been treated wrongfully by your employer and have retained a lawyer, most employment lawyers will begin an investigation of your potential legal claims before providing advice on whether it makes sense to file a lawsuit. This may involve obtaining information from your employer, interviewing potential witnesses, filing a required administrative charge with a state or federal agency, and/or negotiating an early settlement with your employer.

Depending on the results of a lawyer's investigation into your potential claims and efforts to resolve your concerns without filing a lawsuit, the next step is deciding whether to file suit.

Filing a Lawsuit: What Can I Expect?

Filing a lawsuit in state or federal court begins with the filing of a complaint and paying a required filing fee. Once that is done, the long road of litigation begins.

The next step in most jurisdictions is a conference with the judge assigned to your case, during which a schedule will be established for the course of the litigation. Dates will be set for completion of discovery, the filing of any dispositive motions, other key deadlines, and the trial itself.

"Discovery" is a process by which parties to litigation can gain information from the other party and third parties. The usual discovery methods are interrogatories (written questions you and your employer can ask of each other), document requests (you and your employer may request relevant documents from each other), and depositions (essentially, oral interviews by each party's lawyer of potential witnesses under oath and transcribed by a private court reporter). Discovery usually lasts several months.

Dispositive motions are particularly common in employment litigation after completion of discovery, and are critical to your case. Under state and federal rules, the employer may file a motion for "summary judgment" that asks the judge to dismiss the case before it is heard by a jury. These motions are almost always filed by the employer (it is exceedingly rare for an employee to file such a motion), and your lawyer has an opportunity to file a written memorandum in opposition to the motion. The judge reviews these motions and makes a decision whether the case will even proceed to trial. This aspect of the litigation usually takes several months as well.

Only after the judge denies an employer's motion for summary judgment are you entitled to a trial. Many cases are scheduled for trial at least 18 months after they are filed, although the speed of the litigation depends upon the particular jurisdiction in which you file suit.

In short, litigation is time consuming, stressful, and involves some out-of-pocket costs. Always obtain an estimate from your lawyer of such costs, as well as the expected length of the litigation.

Tip: Increasingly, discovery includes electronic discovery by which parties can obtain copies of e-mails, text messages, instant messages, social media postings, and voice mails. Thus, if you are contemplating or are already involved in litigation, be aware that your seemingly private electronic communications may be subject to review by your opponent.

Why Would I Settle for Less Than What a Jury Might Award?

Employment cases in litigation are either dismissed by the judge or settled over 90 percent of the time. The likeliest outcome of a lawsuit is a negotiated settlement for something less than what a successful jury verdict would provide. Why?

The simple answer is that any employment litigation involves a risk of loss. Depending on the facts of your case, your case may be dismissed by the judge, you may lose at trial, or you may lose on appeal. Unfortunately for employees, you must win the fight over a motion for summary judgment, you must win the trial, and you must win a likely appeal to collect a jury verdict. On the other hand, if your employer wins one of these battles, you lose and collect nothing. In some ways, the deck is stacked in favor of your employer.

One advantage that you may have in litigation is that you may only have to pay legal fees if you are successful (assuming your lawyer takes the case on a contingency fee arrangement). In contrast, your employer will likely be paying its lawyer by the hour and litigation can be very expensive.

Depending on your tolerance for risk, you should almost always consider a settlement. As the saying goes, "A bird in the hand is worth two in the bush."

What are "Mediation" and "Arbitration"?

Cases are generally settled in one of three ways: direct negotiations between the lawyers, a settlement conference conducted by the judge, or mediation. A successful settlement requires both parties to compromise.

Your lawyer will almost always try to negotiate directly with the other side after receiving your authority to initiate discussions. This is the most common way to explore settlement.

Alternatively, some courts will become involved in settlement discussions by scheduling a settlement conference, conducted by the judge assigned to the case or another judge or magistrate. Some judges become actively involved, whereas others prefer not to be part of settlement discussions.

The third, increasingly common form of settlement discussions involves a court-appointed mediator (provided free of charge to the parties) or a private mediator (hired by the parties). Mediation is voluntary, and a mediator *assists* the parties who are attempting to determine whether a settlement is possible. A mediator does not decide what manner of settlement makes sense; the parties make that decision.

In contrast, if you arbitrate your claims (usually only if your company has required you to agree to a mandatory arbitration process before or during your employment), a professional arbitrator *decides* your case rather than a jury. The process is similar to a jury trial, though less formal, but the arbitrator plays the role of judge and jury if you are not able to settle your case before the trial. Most employment lawyers representing employees oppose mandatory arbitration and prefer that their clients have a right to a jury trial.

Tip: *A good settlement, it is often said, is one in which both parties are equally unhappy. That is, both parties compromise more than they initially desired to compromise. The good news is that any settlement will result in getting something rather than "throwing the dice" and possibly losing altogether. Always remember that settlement is your decision, not your lawyer's. A good lawyer will advise you on any proposed settlement, and you should consider that advice carefully in making your decision.*

What Happens if I Don't Settle My Case?

If you don't settle your case and it is not dismissed by the judge prior to trial, your case will likely proceed to a trial by jury as do most employment disputes that reach this point. In federal court, juries must decide the case unanimously; in some states, less than unanimity is required, with often just an affirmative vote by three-quarters of the jurors.

If you win your case, the company will have a right to appeal. Often, settlement discussions are renewed before an appeal is filed and, if those efforts are unsuccessful, will continue during the appeal process. An appeal involves a review of the decision by an appellate court, which will consider what happened during the trial. This process can take several months and often longer than a year.

An appeals court can uphold a verdict, modify a verdict, reverse a verdict, or order a new trial.

Part 10

Epilogue

Our Random Justice System: Why Similar Cases Can End Up Very Differently

If you find yourself questioning whether you should file a legal claim in a state or federal court, you should understand the reality that the American system of justice, while still the best in the world, is nowhere close to perfect and, in fact, is disturbingly random.

The legal system is flawed in the sense that not all wrongs are recognized, and not all victims receive a just result. It helps to think of the legal system as a process of dispute resolution that provides most people with a chance of some sort of closure to their dispute. The process relies on fallible human beings to resolve complex matters, and people perceive justice in diverse ways.

By the very nature of the process, not all victims receive justice. In fact, most cases end with each side to the dispute being unhappy. Many judges, in fact, believe that a good resolution occurs when both sides are *equally* unhappy.

The legal system that governs employment situations is somewhat arbitrary. Identical employment cases do not bear identical results, and many people with "good" cases who deserve a "good" result often do not receive as much "justice" as other individuals with worse cases. Why? The reasons are multiple, and spring from fundamental misunderstandings about what it takes to receive justice.

Many different factors affect whether justice is achieved, including the following:

- Who is your lawyer, and how qualified is she?
- Who is the company's lawyer, and how qualified is she?
- Can you afford the time and expense of litigation and handle the associated stress?
- In which court system should you file your lawsuit?
- Which judge is assigned to your case?
- If you have a jury trial, who are the jurors who will decide your case?

In our judicial system, the only factor you will control in most cases is the first one: Who is your lawyer? For that reason, you should never simply defer to someone else's idea as to who is right for you. In most instances, it is worthwhile spending the time and money necessary for you to choose the best available lawyer for your situation.

It is no coincidence that, as has been conveyed throughout this book, a host of federal, state, and local laws has been enacted to address myriad employment issues that significantly undermine the employment-at-will doctrine spawned in the 19th century—a doctrine still wrongly espoused as if employees enjoy few, if any, rights in the workplace. Concerns about employment are of great importance because, for most of us, work will encompass at least one-third of our adult life until retirement. Given the inevitable fact that fallible humans must fill the challenging roles of employer and employee, it is no wonder that a lot can go wrong in the work environment. Sometimes employers mean well and unintentionally do wrong. Sometimes they harbor ill will toward their employees and act accordingly. And, while this book has focused mostly on the wrongdoing of employers, sometimes employees are in the wrong.

In any event, if you are a prospective, current, or former employee, it pays to know your rights and to be aware of what to do if problems develop related to your employment. This book has acquainted you with the scope of your rights, responsibilities, and protections as an employee, and has informed you of the many ways you can navigate the stormy waters of employment disputes.

Author's Note

It is my wish that, someday, all employers will treat their employees with the dignity and respect they deserve, and that employment lawyers will need to find another line of work.

I hope that this book will contribute to your success in whatever occupation you pursue, and that you will not need to retain a lawyer to represent you.

Randy Freking